SCOTNOTES

Number 35

KU-350-032

Ena Lamont Stewart's

Men Should Weep

John Hodgart

Association for Scottish Literary Studies 2015

Published by
Association for Scottish Literary Studies
Scottish Literature
7 University Gardens
University of Glasgow
Glasgow G12 8QH
www.asls.org.uk

ASLS is a registered charity no. SC006535

First published 2015

Text © John Hodgart

All rights reserved. No part of this book may be
reproduced, stored in a retrieval system, or
transmitted in any form or means, electronic,
mechanical, photocopying, recording or otherwise,
without the prior permission of the
Association for Scottish Literary Studies.

A CIP catalogue for this title
is available from the British Library

ISBN 978-1-906841-25-6

CONTENTS

SCOTNOTES

Study guides to major Scottish writers and literary texts

Produced by the Education Committee
of the Association for Scottish Literary Studies

Series Editors
Lorna Borrowman Smith
Ronald Renton

Editorial Board
Ronald Renton
(Convener, Education Committee, ASLS)
Craig Aitchison
Jim Alison
Gillin Anderson
Laurence Cavanagh
Professor John Corbett
Dr Emma Dymock
Dr Maureen Farrell
Dr Morna Fleming
Professor Douglas Gifford
John Hodgart
Bob Hume
Catrina McGillivray
Ann MacKinnon
Dr David Manderson
Dr Christopher Nicol
Lorna Ramsay
Professor Alan Riach
Dr Christine Robinson
Lorna Borrowman Smith

THE ASSOCIATION FOR SCOTTISH LITERARY STUDIES aims to promote the study, teaching and writing of Scottish literature, and to further the study of the languages of Scotland.

To these ends, the ASLS publishes works of Scottish literature; literary criticism and in-depth reviews of Scottish books in *Scottish Literary Review*; short articles, features and news in *ScotLit*; and scholarly studies of language in *Scottish Language*. It also publishes *New Writing Scotland*, an annual anthology of new poetry, drama and short fiction, in Scots, English and Gaelic. ASLS has also prepared a range of teaching materials covering Scottish language and literature for use in schools.

All the above publications are available as a single 'package', in return for an annual subscription. Enquiries should be sent to:

ASLS
Scottish Literature
7 University Gardens
University of Glasgow
Glasgow G12 8QH

Tel/fax +44 (0)141 330 5309
e-mail **office@asls.org.uk**
or visit our website at **www.asls.org.uk**

Page references are given firstly to the 7:84 Edition (out of print) and secondly to the Samuel French edition.

1. THE AUTHOR AND HER WORK

Ena Lamont Stewart was born in the Anderston district of Glasgow in 1912, the youngest of nine children. Her father was a minister whose parish was in one of the poorest districts of the city and she certainly knew from an early age what it was like growing up in a large family where luxuries were few. Yet she regarded herself as fortunate to have grown up in a happy and relatively prosperous home in comparison to most industrial working-class families, many of whom lived on the breadline, especially during the hungry thirties when millions of men were unemployed. As a young girl, Stewart was deeply affected by the poverty she saw around her in the city, particularly in the Gorbals, and one of her abiding memories was the sight of working-class 'shawly women' fighting their way into her father's jumble sales, desperately seeking bargains. (*The Shawlie* was the title of a 1920s play by Robin Miller set in the slums of the Cowcaddens.)

Unfortunately her father died when she was only sixteen and she had to leave school to find work, firstly as a librarian in Aberdeen and then as a receptionist in Glasgow's Sick Children's Hospital where she witnessed at first hand the dire effects of poverty and malnutrition on the health of the city's children. Apparently the harrowing experiences she encountered there had such a profound effect on her that she virtually felt compelled to write about them, especially in one of her first plays *Starched Aprons,* the title of which refers to the nurses' uniforms of the day. In fact many of her actual experiences in the hospital were to resurface in her plays, such as the time a distraught mother asked her for some brown paper to make a parcel for her child's clothes because 'they've kep him in', a painful experience recounted by Maggie Morrison in *Men Should Weep.*

Ena married the actor Jack Stewart with whom she had a son, though they later divorced. It was through Stewart that she was introduced to Glasgow's theatre world and he was in fact one of the actors who played the part of John Morrison in the first version of *Men Should Weep* between 1947 and 1948. Both Ena and her husband joined MSU

1

Repertory Theatre, Rutherglen, (named after its founder Molly
S. Urquhart) which gave her some acting experience and
later produced her first work in 1942, a one-act play called
Distinguished Company.

Her husband later worked for the Glasgow Unity Theatre,
a company formed by the amalgamation of various amateur
drama groups consisting of mainly working-class actors who
wanted

> a theatre indigenous to the people of Glasgow in particular,
> and Scotland in general ... to create a native theatre, some-
> thing which is essentially reflecting the lives of the ordinary
> people of Scotland.

They also declared their aim of presenting

> side by side with the best works of international literature
> as many new and virile Scottish plays as we can find.

A key element in their approach was to portray Scottish
working-class life as realistically as possible – as in the works
of writers like James Barke or Joe Corrie, both of whom wrote
several plays for the group using language and a style that
would certainly not be found in the rather predictable menu
of frivolous romantic comedies and bourgeois drawing-room
dramas which dominated mainstream theatre at that time.
Lamont Stewart also felt alienated by what she often saw in
the 'respectable' theatre of her day:

> One evening in the winter of 1942 I went to the theatre. I
> came home in a mood of red-hot revolt against cocktail time,
> glamorous gowns and underworked, about-to-be deceived
> husbands. I asked myself what I wanted to see on stage and
> the answer was Life. Real Life. Real People.

In contrast to what they saw as essentially a bourgeois
theatre, Unity were very much committed to dramatising the
suffering of the working class with the kind of gritty realism
we now associate with more recent Scottish novels or films,

but presenting it from a left-wing political viewpoint that showed how heavily the odds were stacked against the poorest members of society, while also celebrating the human qualities that helped them to survive. Their motto, printed on all their programmes, was taken from the Russian revolutionary writer Maxim Gorky and his views on Socialist Realism:

> The theatre is the school of the people, it makes them think and it makes them feel.

In reacting against the respectable theatre of their time they were clearly influenced not only by Gorky but by Irish drama, especially the work of Sean O'Casey whose tragi-comic dramas, depicting Dublin slum life during and after the First World War, explored the tensions and violent hatreds of a bitterly divided country, but deployed a vigorous earthy dialogue that very much celebrated the richness of the city's racy language, something that clearly inspired Stewart.

Stewart's passionate reaction to what she witnessed in the theatre in 1942 stimulated her into writing her second play, *Starched Aprons*, a slice of life drama based on her experience of the city's children's hospital, which focused particularly on the nurses' struggle with long hours in very trying and difficult circumstances. However it was not until her husband gave a copy of the play to Unity Theatre's artistic director, Robert Mitchell, that it was produced by Glasgow Unity Theatre in 1945 and proved tremendously popular.

> She ... just recorded her experiences, the people coming into the reception and the attitudes of the nurses, doctors, the disciplinarian system which was in vogue at the time with the matrons and sisters, who were real dragons. (Robert Mitchell)

Starched Aprons was in fact Unity Theatre's first really successful play and toured to Edinburgh and to the Embassy Theatre, London. However, their greatest success was Robert McLeish's *The Gorbals Story* which became such a smash hit that it was seen by possibly around 100,000 across the country in its first year and was also performed in London and even filmed. The starkly realistic picture of slum life it portrayed held a huge appeal, especially for those who had first-hand experience of living in the slums, in effect drawing many people to the theatre who had probably never seen a play before.

As a result of this success Stewart was commissioned to write another work which would reflect more of women's experience of life in the slums and which she apparently wrote with such passion over two days that it turned out to be her greatest achievement:

> I couldn't possibly tell you what I was thinking about when I sat down to write it ... I wrote *Men Should Weep* at such a pitch of intensity I had no idea what the characters were going to do next ... I think it was a kind of emotional release I needed at the time.

The original title of this play was in fact *Poor Men's Riches*, though it was soon changed to *Men Should Weep*. It was first performed by Unity Theatre at the Athenaeum Theatre on 30 January 1947 followed by a highly acclaimed tour across Scotland and then to London between 1947 and 1948. This amply demonstrated that Unity Theatre had a talented new dramatist in their midst and a play that was a theatrical landmark in the representation of Scottish working-class life and the role of women in particular. Considering that the play was so deeply rooted in Glasgow and voiced in the language of the slums, it was really quite remarkable that the play was performed in London (June 1948) but what is even more astonishing is that it was generally well received by the critics.

David Lewin from the *Daily Express* could hardly have been more enthusiastic:

> I didn't understand a quarter of the Glasgow Unity Players' Scots dialect in last night's human tragedy from Glasgow's East side. But I loved every minute of it.

When it returned to Glasgow in August of that year, Robert McLellan, a very distinguished Scottish dramatist, wrote:

I don't think I have been so moved by anything in the theatre since I saw the Abbey Theatre (Dublin), then at the height of its powers, in *The Plough and the Stars.*

To be compared to one of Sean O'Casey's greatest plays was high praise indeed.

Although written from a left wing political perspective, these post war Unity plays were not simply 'agit-prop' theatre (agitation-propaganda) which lectured to the audience about the evils of Capitalism and offered a Socialist alternative, usually presenting the working class in a very stereotypical and usually heroic manner as a powerful force for social and political change. While their post-war plays did celebrate the positive aspects of ordinary working-class people, particularly their courage, common sense, warmth and humour, they also did not hide from the less admirable, often self-inflicted problems of industrial working-class life, such as alcoholism, violence, sectarianism and bigotry.

However, the most significant difference was that these post war plays were much more focused on the working classes as individual human beings struggling with the everyday problems of family life and relationships during the depression era, rather than simply dealing with the working class en masse in a depersonalised manner. In this way they were much more successful in giving a voice to the poorest section of society, the industrial urban working class and within that group, the most marginalised of all, the working-class female voice. These were the voices that were least likely to be heard in 'respectable' theatre of the period, unless when being caricatured as figures of fun.

Undoubtedly Stewart's vigorous scripts, especially in *Men Should Weep,* let her audience see and hear sharply observed convincing characters who spoke the language of the streets and the tenements with an explosive vitality, a tradition already established in popular or political Scottish drama, especially in the plays of Joe Corrie about working-class mining communities. Stewart's work was challenging in both content and style and in many respects she was also at least a decade ahead of the so-called 'angry young men' and kitchen sink dramas and films of the 1950s in England. As Jack Tinkler of the *Daily Mail* wrote in his review of the 1982 revival:

> Less kindly mortals would have every right to feel bitter that the acclaim given to the school of Angry Young Men in the Fifties had actually been pre-empted by the writings of this Gentle Middle-Aged Woman ten years previously.

Unfortunately, instead of being given support and time to develop her work, Lamont Stewart was sadly thwarted in her theatrical ambitions. Her subsequent plays were turned down, one apparently so vehemently by the famous Scottish dramatist, Osborne Henry Mavor (better known by his penname of James Bridie, founder member and director of the Citizens Theatre) that she ran home in despair and tore up all the copies. He was the very man who might have been expected to encourage her talent but allegedly he told her in no uncertain terms that her plays would never be performed at the Citizens.

It was almost as if she had briefly intruded into an exclusive theatre club for respectable and scholarly gentlemen who were now showing her the door, maybe because she was too closely associated with the political theatre of Unity, as opposed to the more bourgeois-centred dramas preferred by the theatrical establishment who saw such work as too directly political or propagandist for their liking. And she was also a woman! But not only that: she was a woman who used dramatic language that was much too 'common' for many of the Citizens' more genteel patrons of that time!

There may have been other reasons, but sadly she was never given the chance to develop her full dramatic potential as her scripts were repeatedly rejected or ignored and she spent many years struggling to make ends meet. Yet her painfully frustrated career was not unusual for Scottish dramatists of the time, male or female, as other talented writers also struggled to ensure that authentic Scottish voices were heard in the mainstream theatre, something that had to wait for another generation or so.

Her other plays performed around this time (early 1950s) were *The Heir to Ardmally* and *Kind Milly* (Pitlochry Festival Theatre), *Walkies Time for a Black Poodle* (Edinburgh Netherbow and Pitlochry Theatre and adapted for radio in 1975–76) and *Knocking on the Wall* (Edinburgh Festival). Other works were either turned down or never saw the light of day.

Partly as a result of her experience she became a founder member, along with Joan Ure and Ada F. Kay, of both the Scottish League of Dramatists and the Scottish Society of Playwrights. Yet in spite of her greatest work being virtually forgotten for over thirty years, Ena Lamont Stewart lived long enough to enjoy the tremendous success of a revived *Men Should Weep* from the early 1980s onward and also to see some of her other works performed. Although she suffered from Alzheimer's disease in her later years, she still lived to the ripe old age of ninety-four. She died in Dalmellington, Ayrshire in 2006.

2. INTRODUCTION TO
MEN SHOULD WEEP

Men Should Weep should really be regarded as a work which evolved over a long period of time. After Unity Theatre closed in the early 1950s the play fell into obscurity and did not see the light of day for about another twenty odd years, something that now appears quite hard to credit. Though Stewart rewrote the ending of the play in 1976, it was not until it was rediscovered in the early 1980s by John McGrath of the 7:84 Theatre Company that it was performed again. It is this latter version that was hailed as almost a lost masterpiece and which has become something of a Scottish theatre classic, now widely studied in English and Drama courses.

Its revival in 1982 by 7:84 (as part of its Clydebuilt Season), directed by Giles Havergal of the Citizens Theatre, restored Stewart's reputation and the production was such a success that Elizabeth MacLennan, who played the lead role, later wrote:

> Every national paper had acclaimed her (Stewart) from the *Wall Street Journal* to the *Aberdeen Evening News*. (*The Moon Belongs to Everyone*, Methuen, 1990).

The revival also opened the play up to a whole new generation on whom it made such a deep impression that in 1998 when theatre professionals were asked to nominate the best twentieth century English language plays, among the one hundred plays selected was *Men Should Weep* representing the year 1947. In 2005, after another production by the Citizens' Theatre, it was rated one of the top fifty plays of the last century.

What many people, who saw the play for the first time in the early 1980s, wanted to know was where this play had come from as most people then had never even heard of Ena Lamont Stewart. What puzzled many even more was why such a powerful play had been forgotten or overlooked as few people then seemed to know about it and even David Hutchison's history of the Scottish theatre published in the 1977 did not mention it. The reason for this is partly due to her neglect by the Scottish theatre establishment of the fifties, which has already been discussed, but it is also due to the fact that the play as we know it today is quite a different one from the original production by Glasgow Unity Theatre. Although the new version still contained much of the original, especially its humour, the original ending was extremely grim, harrowing and melodramatic.

Yet although the original play was much less satisfactory in many ways, we shouldn't forget that the 1947–48 production was still highly acclaimed. Indeed some of the original cast did not like the changes that were made to the play for its revival, many of them agreeing with Elspeth Cameron (who played the part of Mrs Harris in the 1947 version) that 'it wasn't our play' any longer. They unquestionably felt that the original play spoke more powerfully about the appalling levels of unemployment, poverty and inequality of the inter-war years as well as reflecting the spirit of post war resolve to build a better, fairer world. Yet apart from the fact that it was now clearly a much changed play, another of the reasons for the great success of the revived production was that the unemployment and poverty caused by the Thatcher Government's policies in the 1980s also revived so many bitter memories of life in the 1930s.

Since then there have been several other productions, including another directed by Havergal for the Citizens' Theatre in 1998. The National Theatre's London production in 2010 and the National Theatre of Scotland's production in 2011 were also highly acclaimed and again many people clearly saw its continuing contemporary relevance in another era of economic crisis and widespread hardship, especially when it could be argued that some politicians seemed intent on making the poorest members of society pay more than their fair share for the country's economic problems.

However, perhaps another highly significant reason for its impact and its contemporary relevance, especially in the revived version in 1982, was due to the fact that Ena Lamont Stewart, (along with Scottish women writers like Catherine Carswell, Willa Muir, Nancy Bryson Morrison, Nan Shepherd,

Ada F. Kay and Naomi Mitchison) was something of a pioneer in the way her drama focuses attention on the pivotal role of women, both within the family and society as a whole and at the same time is also extremely critical of the worst aspects of working-class male chauvinism.

Strange as it may seem to us, some critics of the original 1947 production of *Men Should Weep* were extremely uncomfortable with the feminist aspects of the play and even some of her Glasgow audiences were rather cool in their response to it, possibly because they felt it was far too critical of traditional male values and attitudes. In fact the *Scotsman's* critic commented that

> this is essentially a woman's play, one in which the men – at least in the days of widespread unemployment and the Dole – are fit for nothing but idling, smoking and drinking, varied with a little wife-beating on a Saturday evening.

Even one female critic, Winifred Bannister, writing in the *Daily Express*, felt that

> the bitter vitriolic tirade against the male of the species is its greatest weakness.

Whatever you think of these comments on the original version, there is no doubt that several aspects of the play very much resonated with the growing feminist movement of a younger generation some thirty years later: its sharp focus on the role of working-class women within the family, along with a critical examination of how they are treated by their men, plus (in the revised version) a heroine who attains a new kind of self-discovery.

We can see how the author highlights not only the human cost of poverty, but the tensions it generates within the family and the consequences this has for traditional gender roles if we examine her choice of setting, plot construction, presentation of the main characters, style and staging.

3. SETTING – SOCIAL AND POLITICAL BACKGROUND

Whatever changes were made to the play, both the original and the revised version of *Men Should Weep* undoubtedly present a powerfully authentic picture of a working-class Glasgow family struggling to survive mass unemployment and poverty during what is known as 'the Great Depression' of the 1930s when it seemed that the entire free-market capitalist system was collapsing after the financial crash of 1931. It is set in a crumbling tenement in the East End district of Glasgow, a city that at that time contained some of the worst slum areas in the whole of Europe. They were in effect overcrowded, insanitary warrens, rife with poverty, disease, violence and crime. More than half a million people were crammed into an area of about two or three square miles in the poorest parts of the city.

These intolerable conditions were the direct result of a Victorian industrial legacy that permitted the creation of vast wealth for the privileged few and appalling poverty for the many. In the early twentieth century this level of inequality gave rise to a generation of 'Red' Clydesiders, like John McLean or James Maxton, who fought to create a fairer society through political action, especially during the First World War and the inter-war years. However, it took the social and political effects of the Second World War and a post-war Labour Government to bring about any real changes for the better, especially with the implementation of William Beveridge's plans for a Welfare State.

While our society today has no shortage of problems created by poverty, especially since the financial crash of 2008, it is probably fair to say that we are still relatively protected from the most severe effects of mass unemployment by the Welfare State and because of this we might find it difficult to appreciate the full extent of the widespread dire poverty, deprivation and squalid living conditions of the inter-war years of the twentieth century. At the same time, family size, structures and norms have changed dramatically from the period depicted in the play when the average family was probably around

seven or eight children and it was common for several generations to be living together in very close proximity, often in one
very cramped 'single-end' or two-room tenement flat, usually
without an inside toilet, or at best a toilet shared between
several families on the same floor. Thus people were not only
physically closer for better or worse, but had literally to share
everything from beds to hand-me-down clothes, while mothers
had to stay at home to care for both young and old and the
father's role was to go out to work as the breadwinner.

Even if work could be found, the meagre wages of large
working-class families did not stretch very far, food did not
last long on the table, luxuries were few, if not nonexistent,
and discipline within the home was usually very strict, often
dispensed with a heavy hand. On the other hand, there was
often the compensation of growing up surrounded by a community of extended families and supportive neighbours,
whether in close-knit rural or island communities or industrial
areas, like the many mining and mill towns and villages that
covered the landscape at that time, which provided a secure
framework or safety net of strong family bonds and community
loyalties. (See discussion in the **Character and theme** section
about the role of the neighbours in the play.)

Indeed there have possibly been losses as well as gains from
living in a more affluent and privileged society. It has often
been claimed that the prosperity and consumerism of the
second half of the twentieth century has severely eroded if not
destroyed many of the positive values of belonging to such
large families and cohesive communities, as the much smaller
nuclear family has replaced the extended family as the norm.

However, if there is sometimes, on the one hand an element
of distortion and exaggeration in some portrayals of gritty urban
life, especially works of fiction that follow in the 'No Mean City'
tradition, there is also, on the other hand, a tradition of urban
kailyard, of writers looking back on the old tenement communities of their childhood with a strong flavour of rose-tinted
nostalgia for the 'good old days', especially by older people who
maybe only remember the good things about it. We can see
these two contrasting perspectives on tenement life if we
compare 'Where is the Glasgow that I Used to Know' by Adam

McNaughtan and 'Farewell to Glasgow' by Jim McLean, two Glasgow folk songs with totally different opinions about the 'good old days'. Which picture of slum life is closer to Stewart's depiction of tenement life in your opinion? If you have any grandparents who have memories or family stories about those days, try to interview and record what they say. What sort of picture emerges from their memories and does it in any way chime with what you have read in *Men Should Weep*?

Yet ironically after the financial crash of 2008, in yet another era of unemployment, austerity, inequality and falling living standards, it is clear that we have been forced to relearn many of the lessons of the 1930s. Once again we are seeing people struggling to survive in poorly paid part-time jobs or on reduced benefits, or having to depend on food banks or food kitchens as in the 1930s, while the super-rich accumulate vast wealth. Our society today has therefore perhaps more similarity to the society of *Men Should Weep* than it might at first seem, while there is still no shortage of slum areas and starving people in many large cities throughout the world, even in prosperous countries.

To help us feel what it is like to struggle with such hardships at the domestic level, Ena Lamont Stewart brings the full force of 1930s poverty to life onstage by setting the entire action of the play in the Morrisons' cramped and chaotic kitchen. The family live in an overcrowded, crumbling, disease-ridden tenement where sometimes more than ten people occupy a room and kitchen, the parents sleep on the floor, they share a toilet with several other families and their children suffer from diseases like rickets, pneumonia, or tuberculosis, a situation summed up by the Morrisons' eldest daughter, Jenny in Act Three:

> It's rotten, this hoose, Rotten. Damp. Ye ken yersel. It's a
> midden lookin oot on ither middens. It's got rats, bugs ...
> (p. 93, SF, p. 7)

Throughout the play we never leave the Morrisons' kitchen and all the main action takes place onstage before our eyes, with offstage events only serving to reinforce their predicament

or increase the pressure on Maggie and John, such as Alex
and Isa becoming homeless, Bertie being kept in hospital,
or learning about Jenny's struggles to survive on her own.
Likewise, the central character Maggie is only offstage for
short periods as the dramatist sharply focuses our attention
on how the mother of a poor family struggles to hold everything
and everyone together. Both parents and children are shabbily
dressed and always hungry, while Maggie frequently goes
without food so that her husband or children have more to
eat. Stewart thus confronts her audience with the crucial
questions of how families can possibly cope and 'normal' human
relationships can possibly survive when people are reduced
to this level of squalor and human values are under threat
from an obscenely unequal and dehumanising society.

In fact the play was praised far more as a very authentic
social documentary than a drama by some of its earliest critics,
at least one of whom, writing in the *Glasgow Herald* in January
1947, felt it concentrated too much on the former at the expense
of the latter, while the review of the same performance in the
Daily Express, commented:

> Here is a slice of life. It isn't easy to produce. But Mrs Stewart
> hasn't yet given us a play. *Men Should Weep* says nothing
> new, neither presents nor solves problems, but as a social
> document, it should be seen by every citizen.

Whether this comment was entirely fair or not, there is no
doubt that the first audiences were greatly affected by the
vivid and dramatic way that the play dealt with these social
and political issues and this central aspect of the play undoubtedly still carries a powerful impact:

> *Men Should Weep* is one of the best plays ever to be written
> about the corrosive effects of poverty. This is a problem that
> has not gone away. It is the story of people living with the
> pressure of poverty and unemployment today in Glasgow,
> Manchester, London or any city on the planet.
> (Graham McLaren, Director of the National Theatre of
> Scotland production, 2011.)

4. PLOT SUMMARY AND COMMENTARY

Before looking at the plot it might be useful here to summarise the main differences between the earlier and later versions of the play, some of which have already been alluded to.

In the 1947–48 version just about everything that possibly could go wrong does go wrong: Bertie dies in the hospital, Alex murders Isa, Granny ends up in the Poorhouse, Maggie dies in childbirth, Jenny returns home in despair after living as a prostitute, while John, distraught with grief, hits the bottle again as Lily and the neighbours squabble over who knows best about attending to the new born baby and Jenny tries to comfort her father by telling him that she will now care for him but he must sober up and take care of the children for Maggie's sake. Like other Unity plays it highlights the scourge of poverty but its ending is almost a parody of a Victorian Temperance Movement morality drama presenting us with a catalogue of tragedies, all due to the evils of the demon drink. In the revised version, Alex fails to kill Isa, Bertie and his mother both survive, she does not become pregnant and, when Jenny surprisingly returns home at the end, John is shamed by his wife into accepting their daughter's kind offer of paying their rent for a good flat in a nice part of the city, and he only has to come to terms with Maggie's new-found resolve instead of resorting to the demon drink.

By examining the plot structure of the play we can see how the drama concentrates on the pressures exerted on the family as a whole and the individual members of it. Although the subject matter, presentation and language of the play were in many ways ground-breaking, the plot structure is fairly conventional in following the familiar three act drama structure of exposition, development towards crisis and climax, a pattern repeated across each act, while the final scene leads us to the ultimate climax of the play and a partial resolution at the end.

Act One, Scene One dramatises the hectic events in the Morrison household one winter evening, beginning with the usual struggle of Maggie Morrison to put her children and their Granny to bed, in the midst of which her unmarried sister, Lily, arrives to offer help and 'advice' on how to bring up a family and create some order in Maggie's chaotic household. Yet only a few moments later Lily ironically contradicts her own criticisms of 'the midden' her sister is living in, as she vehemently defends Maggie when her husband, John, arrives to add his critical 'advice', that 'women have nae system'. It is immediately evident that there is a history of friction between John and Lily and that John cannot help trying to have his joke at her expense, something we soon see when she takes exception to John's cruel jibe about her desperation for a man, thereby causing her to stomp out, warning that they will get no more help from her until John's manners improve.

When we hear their son Bertie coughing offstage, we realise that Maggie is reluctant to take him to the hospital for an x-ray but she promises John that she will ask one of the neighbours to go with her soon. When the neighbours arrive at the end of the scene with their dramatic news of the collapsed building, in which the Morrisons' son Alex and his wife Isa were living, the main action of the play is set in motion. Alex and Isa are in fact now homeless and we can see that Maggie will end up taking them into her already overcrowded home, much against John's wishes. Unfortunately Maggie then quarrels with Mrs Harris over cleaning the stair and also the small matter of lice on the children's heads, which will mean having to appease her later with food offerings, something that is scare enough in the Morrison household as we see from the way John and Maggie savour Lily's present of a tin of beans.

Although most of the domestic arguments are humorous and seem quite mundane and trivial, they actually play an important part in introducing all the main conflicts and characters, especially the differing perspectives on marriage and men, as well as introducing the Morrisons' worries about daughter Jenny and foreshadowing the problems of their son Alex and his wife Isa, plus establishing the mood and theme of the play. The mood at the start is fairly light-hearted and essentially humorous, with even the dramatic news of the collapsed building being quite comical, but there are sparks of tension in the air between several characters and there are darker undercurrents just below the surface.

Scene Two, the shortest in the play, then develops the Morrisons' worries regarding their two eldest children, concerns first raised by Lily in Scene One. When John arrives with the intoxicated Alex and his tipsy wife, we immediately see that much of what Lily said of them might well be true and we also soon realise that the shiftless Alex and his brazen wife Isa will only bring problems of a more serious nature to the Morrisons' home, especially when we learn that they are penniless as well as homeless. As Alex and Isa crawl into whatever spaces they can find in the children's beds, John and Maggie make up their own bed on the floor and discuss their worries about their children, to the background accompaniment of Bertie's constant consumptive cough, offstage, but their more immediate worry is about their eldest daughter Jenny who has taken to 'tarting' herself up, keeping 'bad' company and returning home very late. When she is heard giggling in the close below with a boyfriend, her father is so enraged that he embarrasses her by dragging her upstairs and this leads to a violent quarrel during which he strikes her when she taunts him with her plans to quit her job and leave home, a place she describes as a 'rotten pig-sty'.

Act Two, Scene One opens a week later when Maggie is away at the hospital with her young son Bertie and the neighbours are watching the rest of the children as well as Granny who is waiting to be collected by her mercenary daughter-in-law, Lizzie. The latter is resentful at having to take Granny before her turn is due and when Lily arrives she is just in time to help the neighbours put Lizzie in her place and prevent her removing food from the cupboard, something she feels entitled to because Granny's pension has already been drawn by Maggie. When Isa and Jenny return to add their 'clever' comments to the row, another series of verbal battles break out between the two younger women and Lily who is supported firstly by the neighbours and then the removal man who soon puts Isa firmly in her place over the way she speaks to Granny.

As the old woman reluctantly prepares to leave, Maggie returns disconsolately from the hospital with the news that

Bertie has tuberculosis (often fatal in those days) and has been 'kep in.' At this point the exhausted Maggie seems like someone in a daze, oblivious even to Granny's departure and only rouses herself when she realises that Jenny is about to leave home. She pleads desperately with her daughter to stay, but Jenny is quite resolved and when her father returns she leaves quickly with hardly a word to her parents. This scene ends with John's utter dejection and sense of failure at being thus rejected by his eldest daughter and personal favourite. By the end of Scene One, the mood has darkened considerably and the Morrisons' problems have clearly intensified, but things only go from bad to worse in the next scene.

Act Two, Scene Two first concentrates on Alex's problems: his sycophantic relationship with the ruthless Isa and the effect of this on his parents, especially Maggie. Alex, increasingly desperate for money to stop Isa leaving him, has now turned to mugging, though his lack of success leads to another violent quarrel. When Maggie returns home in the middle of all this, Alex feigns illness in an attempt to win his mother's sympathy, something he almost succeeds in as she suddenly turns on Isa, striking her when she calls her 'a dirty auld bitch'. At this point John enters and sorely disappoints his wife, not only by turning against her and even threatening her, but by actually siding with Isa, who then tries flirting with him when Maggie exits. If the previous scene ends with John at his lowest point emotionally, this scene draws to a very tense close with Maggie running from the house in tears on discovering that young Ernie's new boots are worn through, a seemingly trivial problem, but, as she is almost penniless, it is too much for her to bear at this point.

This unexpected outburst is the culmination of having returned home exhausted from her cleaning jobs to find, ironically, her own house in a mess and nobody having lifted a finger to help, plus the ensuing rows, especially John's uncharacteristically violent language towards her. Yet in spite of all this, she returns to apologise to John a few minutes later while he is busy trying to reassure their frightened children and 'organise' the tea. Thus family life returns to normal, at least on the surface, but Maggie's painful joke about the meaning of 'heartburn' betrays how she really feels. Even at her lowest point, Maggie manages to put her own feelings aside and to pull herself together for the sake of her family. The pace has quickened, the tension has heightened and the mood has darkened considerably in this scene with the under-lying conflicts all coming to a head in a key confrontation which provides crucial moments of revelation.

Act Three presents us with an unexpected transformation in the family's fortunes and in the mood of the play. Order has replaced disorder in the Morrison household as John has acquired a job and is determined to give his family the best Christmas they have ever had. They now possess 'a wireless' (i.e. radio, the new must-have gadget of the 1930s) to the delight of young Ernie, while Granny is happily restored to her rocking chair, as at the beginning of the play. The neighbours share in their celebrations over tea and cake and a warm party atmosphere soon develops, a happiness symbolised by the bright red hat John has bought Maggie as a Christmas present. However, Alex's return soon sours the festive atmosphere and once everyone else has gone out, the mood changes abruptly to something we might expect from a Victorian melodrama, a scene that could potentially take a tragic turn, as he tries unsuccessfully to strangle Isa in a desperate attempt to stop her leaving him, though as usual she manages to outwit him.

Following this grim scene there is again a sudden change of mood in a brief interlude of great tenderness between Lily and Maggie, on their return from Christmas shopping, before Jenny, well dressed and prosperous looking, returns unexpect-edly, like a prodigal and dutiful daughter, to offer her mother financial help with moving to a good house in a better part of the city until they get a new council house. Bertie could then return home and recover properly from tuberculosis, though his mother has been concealing the fact that he will only be allowed out of hospital if he has a better place to stay. Lily is initially sarcastic and fault-finding, but Maggie welcomes her daughter, and her offer, with open arms.

However, when John returns, his pride and bitterness against Jenny will not allow him to accept help from a source he regards as 'whore's winnins'. His resistance is only broken when Maggie, determined to accept Jenny's help, is driven to humiliate John by exposing his sexual hypocrisy. As he sits weeping, the play ends with Lily gloating over John's defeat, Jenny trying to express her love for him and seeking forgiveness, while Maggie looks forward longingly to her vision of a better future in a new home free from squalor and poverty, though there may be other less tangible changes that Maggie also longs for and not only the flowers they might see in the nearby park come spring.

The understated simplicity of her final lines really says much more than the actual words, like the final lingering notes of a very moving song or piece of music:

> I can manage him ... I can aye manage him ... *(Very softly)*
> Four rooms, did ye say, Jenny *(Pause)* Four rooms. Four
> rooms ... an a park forbye! There'll be flowers come the spring!
> (p. 96, SF, p. 74)

'There'll be flowers come the spring' might seem a rather clichéd last line, but its simplicity speaks volumes about how thrilled Maggie is at the possibility of living in a decent house with a park nearby, something that would seem like a paradise to a Glasgow slum dweller of that time and would indeed be the best present a woman in Maggie's position could ever imagine.

The return home of the 'lost' member of the family, the prodigal son (as in the biblical parable) or in this case the daughter, is a stock situation from the old melodramas of stage and screen and we should also bear in mind the references to the Christmas tree fairy, but we are still far from a fairy-tale happy-ever-after ending here. Arguably the bitter rows which develop, firstly with Lily, secondly between Jenny and her father, then finally between John and Maggie keep this final climatic scene free from sentimentality and true to the realistic treatment of the play as a whole. How far do you agree or disagree that the revised ending is too good to be true? Are you convinced that Maggie will ensure they take up Jenny's offer and that things will work out as she hopes?

Character and theme will be discussed at greater length later, but, bearing the plot changes in mind, perhaps you may want to consider here how far you agree with the critic who said that 'this is essentially a woman's play' and whether you accept that 'the bitter vitriolic tirade against the male of the species' (see critical comments in the Introduction above) is still an issue even in the revised version or whether the author in fact succeeds in achieving a better balance in this version. Also consider who voices the most critical comments on the male of the species and why she makes them and how far the behaviour and attitudes of the male characters support or refute this viewpoint.

Perhaps you might also want to think here about whether or how far you agree that the changes make for a better play overall and whether or how far you can sympathise with some of the original cast who did not like the changes that were made. Possibly you might feel there are strengths and weaknesses to both endings, but how far do you accept the view that in many ways the new ending is a more fitting and logical conclusion to many of the key conflicts at the heart of the plot, especially the tensions between Maggie, John and Lily, as well as providing a much more positive and satisfactory culmination to Maggie's character development?

If we compare the very negative ending of the original with the much more positive outcome of the revised version, you might, firstly, consider that the earlier version contained so many disasters that it lacked credibility and, secondly, left us with such a dark ending that it simply drowns the play in misery and even abandons the central conflicts of the drama. In addition the earlier version arguably vindicates Lily's bitter and warped view of men and marriage, as all the pain and misery is inflicted by irresponsible or feckless men, hence the criticisms made by Winifred Bannister in the *Daily Express* (see Introduction to the play above) that 'the scales are tipped far too heavily in favour of the female', and that 'the strident, nagging female chorus' and the 'author's acid touch' cause many false notes in characterisation, 'turning one's sympathy to embarrassment, even to anger'.

Whether this was entirely fair or not, you may feel that she made a valid point about the original ending at least and perhaps also the overall balance of the play. In contrast, you may feel that the newer version stretches our credibility much less while allowing Maggie's character development to progress to the point of self-realisation and truth in a way that is much more convincing. At the same time, Stewart perhaps creates a far more satisfactory resolution to the play's key conflict and achieves a much better balance between the conflicting perspectives in the play as a whole. Maggie triumphs not by destroying John, only by humiliating him, but she also rejects Lily's jaundiced view of what has happened and so it is Maggie's healthier and more balanced voice that sounds the final positive notes of the drama. This will be discussed further in the character section.

5. CHARACTER AND THEME

If we examine the main characters and their relationships with each other we can see how several contrasting sets of values and attitudes are used to develop the main themes of the play. The unsentimental and honest way it examines relationships between the sexes and between generations is arguably one of the most convincing aspects of the play, while the author's refusal sit in judgement on any of her characters and her balanced treatment of character and themes leaves an audience with much to argue over. As a minor character, **Granny** is dealt with in Chapter 6, **Mood and tone.**

(A) MAGGIE

In spite of all their difficulties, we clearly see at the heart of the Morrison family a genuine love and respect between Maggie and John that has stood the test of time and seven children. Much to Lily's astonishment, Maggie reveals in Act One Scene One that she and John still trust and love each other and early in the next scene she tells John that it is because

> things have aye been right atween you and me that I can struggle on. (p. 31, SF, p. 20)

We are clearly shown that it is this love that provides a mutual source of strength to each other, holding both the family and themselves together.

Perhaps you might consider her view at this point rather sentimental or possibly exaggerated, as if Maggie is maybe over-egging things in her determination to defend herself and her husband against Lily's cynical comments. Stewart shows this love being severely tested by the impact of poverty and the tensions within the family to such an extent that by the end of the play the strength of their relationship has been stretched to breaking point and been altered irrevocably.

Just as their relationship undergoes a profound change, John and Maggie, especially the latter, are also subjected to enormous pressure as individuals. Indeed the normal stresses

23

and strains of bringing up a family are dramatised most effec-
tively throughout the play as we frequently see Maggie trying
to cope with about a dozen things at the same time, such as
when Lily enters near the beginning of the play and passes
Maggie in the kitchen, each hurriedly attending to a different
child. No wonder Lily tells her she doesn't have 'a life fit for a
dog,' because for most of the play she appears very much the
harassed, unappreciated mother, struggling with the never-
ending burden of housework, constantly running after her
children and Granny. She is a woman who sacrifices everything
for her family but proudly defends that as her duty and role
in life against any criticism, especially from her sister Lily.

Maggie also receives little or no help from the other members
of the family with housework, especially her husband, and
when they are temporarily left in Act Two to fend for themselves they really do not know where to start. No wonder she
says there is 'nae work for the men, but aye plenty for the
women,' and she is not referring to paid employment here,
though she is eventually forced to go out cleaning other people's
houses as well as her own. It is, therefore, hardly surprising
that Maggie always looks untidy and bedraggled, in fact older
than she really is – someone who has little or no time for
herself, at least in Acts One and Two. In the opening scene
when Granny is complaining about the night being 'ower
lang' when you are old, Maggie wryly informs her that

> I cannae be as aul as I feel then, for the nicht's a Hell o a
> sight tae short for me; seems I'm nae sooner in ma bed than
> I've tae rise. (p. 7, SF, p. 1)

She has also developed the nervous habit of combing her hair
with her hands when upset or anxious, such as when Bertie's
hospital visits are mentioned, and her sister Lily frequently
has to remind her to use a comb. In spite of her devotion to her
family, there are also occasions in the play where everything
appears to be too much for her to bear, such as when she returns
from the hospital after being told about Bertie's tuberculosis,
or her row with John at the end of Act Two or when she is
worried about what Alex may have done to Isa in Act Three.

On each of the above occasions, however, she eventually finds enough strength to pull herself together and face up to the demands of the situation. Although frequently exhausted, her ability to laugh at herself and her circumstances is clearly an important asset and survival skill, an essential defence mechanism against the pressures to which she is subjected. This is frequently in evidence throughout the play in her handling of Granny, Lily or the neighbours who can sometimes be very helpful, though she can also be very determined in resisting their 'advice' or can be sharp-tongued in putting them in their place. We also see her wry humour in her relationship with John, such as where she makes a joke of his criticism that she has 'nae system' when he cannot find the tin opener. Even when she is at her lowest point emotionally, at the end of Act Two, she soon recovers enough to make a joke, though a very painful and bitter one, about the real meaning of 'heartburn':

> I wonder whit kind o a male idiot called indigestion heartburn? Ma Goad – I could tell him whit heartburn is.
> (p. 65, SF, p. 50)

She is in effect the strongest and most appealing character in the play whose courage, determination and resilience hold the whole family together through the most difficult and painful crises. She very much lives for others, not for herself, and is extremely self-sacrificing towards her children, her love for them being quite unbreakable, regardless of what happens, for as she says herself, it is 'as if they wis tied on tae ye.' When Lily tells her to forget Jenny, her answer is straight from the heart:

> Forget her! It's weel seen you never had a faimly, Lily. Once they've been laid in yer airms, they're in yer heart tae the end o yer days, no maitter whit way they turn oot.
> (p. 81, SF, p. 61)

Yet she is no saintly Madonna, as shown in some of her sharp-tongued exchanges with the neighbours over cleaning

the stairs or the lice-infested hair of Mrs Harris' daughter
Mary, while some might think she deploys a kind of cruel
humour in reply to Granny's litany of woes at the start, though
it is merely teasing banter, or a kind of ironic 'gallus' humour
(laughing at things you are not supposed to, something very
Scottish and certainly very Glaswegian) deployed to make
light of the situation. This is in fact one of Maggie's secret
weapons to help cajole the old woman to bed so that she can
turn her attention to the children, although she soon treats
Granny to a nice cup of tea and a few other sweet treats to
compensate for any unkind words. Granny is in fact much
happier staying with Maggie because she shows her a lot of
kindness in comparison to her sister-in-law Lizzie's mean
attitude towards her.

   Another aspect of Maggie's character that some in a modern
audience might not approve of is that, when she is at the
end of her tether with her children, she resorts, like many
parents of that time, to administering the swift chastisement
of a 'skelp' or even a 'good' leathering. In Act One Scene One
for example she warns Marina in no uncertain terms that if
she spills the jelly from her piece of bread onto the bed, she
will get 'the daein you should have got for spillin yer co-coa
last night' and soon after this, Edie warns Ernest that 'ma's
gonnae wallop the daylights oot o ye' if he does not come in
when he is told and then when Ernie tries to evade being
clouted, Maggie warns him to 'come you here when I want tae
hit ye!' In the context this last example is even quite funny,
perhaps another example of 'gallus' humour, though it might
seem to some people today to be a very tough or cruel way of
disciplining children.

   However, it has to be stressed that these incidents are not
there to present any criticisms of Maggie, or even to reveal
any weaknesses on her part, but only to show us how things
actually were at that time. No doubt this kind of physical
chastisement is a contentious issue today, but we really have
to remember that any exhausted mother in Maggie's position
would have been demented trying to cope with so many noisy,
demanding and hungry children in such a cramped house. To
remind us how this kind of corporal punishment was very

much the norm then, John also occasionally lifts his hands to Ernie, while Lily is very much in agreement with the traditional view of sparing the rod and spoiling the child, especially regarding Maggie's oldest as she feels quite vehemently that Alex has ended up being spoiled by his mother because she 'didnae skelp him enough when he was wee'. Several times in the play we even suspect that Lily would still very much like to skelp him herself and many of the audience might even feel he would deserve it!

Indeed, Maggie is honest enough to recognise that she has pampered her first child Alex far too long and consequently feels responsible for the way he has turned out, possibly taking too much of the blame on herself since she is surely not responsible for a society that offers someone like Alex a chance to make money from petty crime but apparently little chance to earn a living from a decent job. Yet, if she has been too indulgent with Alex, she is possibly over harsh towards his wife, Isa, towards whom she shows signs of maternal suspicion, which are probably justified, but she also perhaps shows traces of jealousy, something Isa certainly suspects. In fact Isa thinks that she has never forgiven her for taking her 'wee boy' away from her, although we are not inclined to accept Isa's viewpoint too readily.

In spite of occasionally losing her temper with her children, or with Isa and John in Act Two, Maggie is usually patient and tactful in handling difficult characters or situations as we see in her relationship with the neighbours or when trying in vain to appease Lily when she is being riled by John in Act One Scene One. These qualities are shown being exercised to the full at the very end of the play when she reassures Jenny by telling her not to be too distressed about her father's tears:

> I can manage him ... I can aye manage him.
> (p. 96, SF, p. 74)

In defence of her role as full-time mother, Maggie responds to Lily's barbed criticisms of marriage and men by telling her that although she is not paid in wages, she is 'paid wi' love'

and that she and John still love each other, a claim that the
acidic Lily treats with scorn. In Act One, Lily is obviously so
angry at seeing her sister struggling to cope that she blurts
out some very barbed comments about John burdening her
with so many children, making her look like a trollop living
in 'this midden,' to which Maggie replies bluntly:

> Ye cannae help havin a midden o a hoose when there's kids
> under yer feet a day. (p. 15, SF, p. 8)

Obviously this is something Lily has little appreciation of.

At one point Maggie even becomes so defensive of the
state of marriage itself that when they hear Mrs Bone once
again being bashed by her husband, she argues that 'when
you've got weans, you've got tae pit up wi the fellow that gie'd
ye them', (p. 20, SF, p. 11) as if in tacit acceptance of the male
vices which Lily is very ready to expose. In this case, Maggie's
opinion sounds rather like condoning whatever aspects of a
man's behaviour a wife finds herself landed with, thus support-
ing the traditional view that marriage is for better or for worse.
Yet in Act Three she makes a comment to Mrs Bone which
offers quite a different perspective on male abuse:

> Ye can close the doors o yer heart on him, and once ye've
> done that tae yer man, batterin wull no get him back in.
> (p. 76, SF, p. 57)

Maggie's honesty also makes her blunt and outspoken when
she has to be, as with Isa in Act Two or with John at the end
of the play, but she is usually the one who tries to soothe over
their differences rather than stirring them up, unlike Lily, for
whom the word appeasement equals surrender. It could be
argued that at some points Maggie appears too tolerant of
some of John's criticisms and behaviour, especially his harsh
words and angry threat to her in Act Two Scene Two, which
drive her close to closing the doors of her heart on him.

Probably the most crucial change from the original version
is that instead of becoming pregnant again and dying in childbirth, the author not only allows Maggie to survive but shows

her as very determined in finally asserting her will to change their lives for the better. In the revised final scene her strength of character is put to its greatest test when, just as Jenny is about to leave, Maggie steps in and displays her courage by exposing John's hypocrisy, thereby forcing him to accept Jenny's offer of help, something that will allow them all the chance of a better future.

Although aspects of the original version were quite daring or even shocking for their time, e.g. Jenny turning to prostitution, John getting Maggie pregnant again and in effect killing her, or the exposure of male fecklessness and wife abuse, Maggie's frank exposure of John's sexual behaviour would almost certainly have been regarded as shocking then and also highly unlikely for a woman of the pre-war period, something Maggie herself alludes to. Yet even with all the greater tolerance and permissiveness of the intervening years, the frankness of Maggie's final outburst still caused some of the audience to feel a degree of discomfort and even a degree of shock thirty-five years later.

Furthermore some even felt that the 'new' Maggie of the revised ending stretched credibility somewhat and that the changes in her character were added to suit the growing feminist discourse of the seventies and eighties. Some have also argued that this change is not altogether consistent with earlier aspects of her character but has been added on to make more of a positive political statement for a different age and a different audience who would be much more approving of this new ending. The author does after all say in the stage directions that Maggie speaks 'with uncharacteristic force' when she asserts 'an so we wull be happy' near the end.

On the other hand, this criticism overlooks the fact that the changes were not altogether out of step with Maggie's character from earlier in the play, as she displays a firm grasp of reality from beginning to end, as well as a rich and resilient sense of humour in coping with her problems, only displaying any bitterness in a moment of great hurt and we see her self-awareness in her ability to face up to the painful truth about her over-indulgence of Alex. Most significantly of all, in Act Two Scene Two, when she is at her lowest ebb, we also see

her challenging John's authority by 'turning on him fiercely'
over what she should spend the money on that she has just
earned from 'skivvying':

Who earned that money? You or me? (p. 62, SF, p. 45)

When John reacts to this challenge 'as if he had been shot',
he slumps into a chair and puts his head in his hands, an
action that surely provides a foreshadowing of the end of the
play. She also puts Lily very firmly in her place in the final
act when she tells her to leave John's present of the red hat
where it is 'with unusual command' when her sister, obviously
disapproving, intended to put it away out of sight. Notice too
that there is dramatic progression in the way scenes end, from
Act One Scene One and Act Two Scene One focusing more on
John's emotional worries and woes (losing Jenny and being
poor) to focusing much more on Maggie at the end of Act Two,
with her acidic joke about 'heartburn', which also in a way
prepares us for the ending.

All of these clearly show that she had already begun
the journey towards self-knowledge and that she certainly
possesses not only the determination but also the necessary
self-realisation to effect positive change. At the end she is
painfully honest about her sexual relationship with John,
though it is maybe questionable whether a woman of that
time or even today, would be so open about this in front of her
family. Yet she also acts in character by immediately regret-
ting her own angry though honest words, clearly feeling that
she has overstepped the mark:

Aw ... aw ... *(She wipes her face with her hands and sighs)*
Aw, I shouldnae have said they things. (p. 96, SF, p. 73)

She also rejects Lily's triumphant assertion that she only
spoke the truth:

(Shaking her head) Naw. There's things atween husbands
an wives that shouldna be spoke aboot. I'm sorry. I lost ma
heid. (p. 96, SF, p. 74)

Yet, also characteristically, she fails to join Jenny in feeling too sorry for John, but instead tells her not to fret as she can manage him, before turning her attention back to the money in her hand and letting her mind's eye focus on the future new house and its leafy surroundings. She has just spoken important truths about the past and said what needed to be said to her husband, but, as she commands the stage at the end, her real triumph is that she has finally asserted herself and is looking forward to a better future for her whole family. Arguably Ena Lamont Stewart also implies in the last line that Maggie is speaking not just about herself but about her whole society emerging from the deprivation of the hungry thirties and the ravages of the war.

Whether you find this new ending convincing or not will ultimately depend on your own reading of her character, but remember at the climax of the play she is in a highly emotional state about Jenny's return and her unexpected offer and is driven almost to an unprecedented level of anger and despair over John's self-righteous intransigence. Unlike John, she is shown to be a realist in accepting Jenny's help and is forgiving enough to understand what Jenny has had to do to save up all this money for them, but she also appreciates that her daughter's love for her family has survived, while John's male pride and hypocritical principles would drive them apart permanently.

Her journey from downtrodden wife and mother to a woman finally asserting her moral authority and making a crucial decision for the welfare of her family is in fact the main trajectory of the drama. Her outburst at the end amounts to a devastating attack on both John's male pride and authority as head of the family and on conventional sexual morality. As his wife, she has brought seven of his children into the world to live in poverty, but that is all right in his eyes, whereas Jenny lives as an unmarried woman with someone who is apparently generous with his money but that is regarded by John Morrison as a 'whore's wages'.

Maggie clearly embodies the author's sympathy and admiration for the many extraordinary mothers of 'ordinary' working-class families. Stewart's portrayal of her also asks some challenging questions about what is expected of women within a traditional working-class Scottish family. At the end we can clearly see that things will never be quite the same again within the family, especially between John and Maggie, but in spite of appearances to the contrary, we must not forget that she could 'aye manage him.' Yet although she achieves a measure of self-determination and independence at the end, Maggie uses her new power not for herself but for the betterment of her family as a whole. Ultimately she is no two-dimensional mythological working-class matriarch of didactic political dramas, but a very convincing flesh and blood indiv-idual, a strong and positive woman who holds her bruised and battered family together throughout everything.

(B) JOHN

In sharp contrast to his wife, who should look older than she really is, John Morrison is described on his entrance in Act One Scene One, as 'a big handsome man' and he still looks young enough for Isa to flatter him with her attentions in Act Two where she tells him that he's 'in his prime' and has 'an air about him.' While we are unlikely to give much credence to what Isa says, his apparent manly authority still appeals to her, especially in contrast to his feckless son, Alex.

When John first enters we should be given the impression of someone trying to maintain a calm paternal authority over a chaotic household, as shown by his aloof criticisms that women have 'nae system', a comment which immediately infuriates Lily but amuses Maggie. We can also see that having to rely on Lily's help clearly irks John's male pride as the breadwinner and head of the family because without her help the family would struggle even more, something John is unwilling to acknowledge, just as he is unwilling to acknowledge the fact that it is really Maggie who holds the family together.

However, unlike the other men in the tenement, he could be seen as representing some of the positive qualities of the traditional Scottish father-figure. Almost like a reformed alcoholic, he will not tolerate alcohol in the house, while, in contrast, other men in the building seek an escape via the bottle and Mrs Bone for one is regularly beaten up by her drunken husband. The neighbouring women regard John Morrison as being exceptional in that he is still honest with his wife and in fact Mrs Harris clearly thinks he is one of the few honest men in their neighbourhood, while Mrs Bone tells Maggie how lucky she is in her man, unlike her own. John still conscientiously tries to find work every day, has given up going to the pub and instead spends much of his time in the library, apparently seeking to further his education or, like many unemployed men, using it as a sort of substitute work-place which provides some kind of daily routine or possibly a sanctuary from his problems or from his wife and family.

Stewart thus portrays John as essentially a responsible caring father whose main concern in life is the welfare of his family and who feels a deep sense of shame at not being able to provide his children with a better life. We are shown how bitterly disappointed he is at how Alex has turned out, though ironically he feels no responsibility for this and in fact at times is severely critical of and unsympathetic towards a bone-idle son he regards as spoiled by his mother (e.g. Act Two Scene Two, p. 62, SF, p. 45). On the other hand, he is deeply hurt by what he sees happening to his eldest daughter Jenny, though he blames her for what he sees as a betrayal of the family. His inability to provide for them is a painful blow to his pride and it is a source of deep personal humiliation to him that Jenny would be ashamed to bring any 'decent fella' to their 'midden' of a house.

Perhaps we might see him as a man whose idea of his own masculinity and status within the community is undermined by the humiliation of unemployment and being forced almost to beg for work. Yet in spite of all these blows to his dignity, he fights hard to retain his personal standards and values, whether we entirely approve of them or not. His personal integrity and honesty are severely tested in Act Two and Act Three, where some of his strengths, but also his weaknesses, are clearly revealed. In spite of the fact that he is sexually provoked by Isa when she flirts with him in Act Two, he still has sufficient control of himself and a firm enough grasp of

reality to resist her charms and give some very honest answers
to her flattery:

> The kids has tae come first. And once ye've a faimly ye begin
> tae forget whit ye used tae look like when ye'd a few bob tae
> spare to posh yersel up ... I've had *nae* prime. I got married.
> Nae trainin. Nae skill; just a labourer when there wis labourin
> needed; and when there's nane ... the Burroo. And there's
> nae escape that I can see. (pp. 64–65, SF, p. 47)

Through this honest appraisal of the realities of his
situation we are given a glimpse into his own lack of
opportunities in life and a sense of his frustration at being
trapped, especially in his own powerlessness to change
anything. Although he takes much for granted, he still
treats his wife with affection and he is still Maggie's 'loving
Johnnie' in spite of Lily's criticisms of her appearance. The
bright red hat he buys Maggie for her Christmas in Act
Three could be seen as a symbol of love surviving all their
difficulties, as Maggie explains how it reminds them of
courting days (though it also highlights Maggie's defiance of
conventional opinion, as she wears it in spite of the disapproval of the other women). When he finally obtains a steady
job by Act Three, his greatest joy is being able to provide for
his family and we are shown his almost boyish delight in
treating them all to Christmas presents, from Maggie's red
hat to Ernie's football boots.

He is, therefore, portrayed as essentially a decent man
almost broken by poverty, a good husband and loving father,
though we are also made fully aware of his faults and short-
coming. Perhaps Stewart is suggesting that even a decent
man, one regarded as a 'good' husband has still much to learn
about his relationship with the women in his life. In spite of
maintaining the pretence of male authority, his stance is
constantly undermined and revealed as being out of touch
with reality. In Act Two Scene Two when he returns home to
find Maggie and Isa quarrelling, he uses extremely harsh
words towards his wife, thus appearing to side with Isa who
has just called Maggie 'a bitch'. When Maggie then protests

about his lack of support after a very hard day's work slaving for others, he uses uncharacteristically threatening language towards her:

> Shut yer mouth or I'll shut it for ye! (p. 61, SF, p. 44)

Maggie is genuinely shocked by this because it is so out of character as he normally treats her with respect and kindness. Yet, like most men of his generation, he regards housework as women's work and would consider himself effeminate if required to do very much in the home:

> Tae Hell wi this Jessie business every time I'm oot o a job!
> I'm no turnin masel into a bloomin skivvy! I'm a man!
> (p. 61, SF, p. 44)

Ironically his wife has had to go out 'skivvying' for others so that her own family can eat, but they still somehow expect her to 'skivvy' for them as well when she comes home. His cruel words and lack of support for his wife at this point are in marked contrast to his apparent sympathy for the sugary-tongued and shiftless Isa and, when Maggie storms out, he blames the children rather than himself for their mother's behaviour and orders them to clear up since it is very obvious he does not really know where to start. When she returns to resume her 'duties', he safely retreats to the pages of his book, relieved that things have apparently reverted to normal and domestic order is being restored.

We are shown very clearly here that he feels little responsibility for what has gone wrong and that he thinks he can now thankfully leave the housework to the women, including his daughter Edie. Thus the author clearly reveals his male arrogance and blindness, treating many of his comments with the comic irony they deserve, especially his claim that women have 'nae system' or his explanation to the children that 'when women gets that tired they kind o loss their heids.' Yet it is the women who restore order to the chaos in his house which he was incapable of dealing with when he also momentarily lost the head.

Undoubtedly his shortcomings are most dramatically high-lighted at the end of the play. As we have already noted, Isa is apparently impressed by his manly authority but his auth-ority as 'head of the house' is repeatedly exposed to ridicule as he really cannot cope without Maggie doing all the domestic drudgery, something he would never lower himself to do. Ironically John's claim in Act Three that 'I'd an idea that I wis heid o this hoose,' is soon exposed as utterly hollow by a series of events within his own household over which he has no authority or control whatsoever.

It is also this false sense of male pride that Maggie has to humiliate at the end as it is a huge obstacle to Jenny's offer of help. His pride and bitterness against his own daughter will not allow him to forgive her and, as head of the family, it is difficult for him to accept that Jenny's money can obtain them a better house than he is able to achieve by honest labour. This is a very bitter pill for him to swallow and we possibly feel sympathy for him up to a point, although we also feel that without Maggie's determined intervention his male ego and his 'principles' would prevent a reconciliation with Jenny and deprive his own children of a better home. He can only accept Jenny's help and forgiveness once Maggie is driven to expose his principles as hypocritical and hollow, thereby humiliating him and deflating his male ego, leaving him broken and silent.

As he sits weeping at the close of the play, we feel that the title of the play applies particularly to him and, because he represents the traditional father-figure of Scottish society, it also has wider implications. We are clearly shown that he now has no option but to accept Maggie's decision to take up Jenny's offer, a decision which finally demonstrates that his attempt to maintain the traditional role as the 'head' of the family has not only been self-deluding but has been potentially damaging to all concerned. Maggie may have helped sustain his illusions but she and Jenny have finally forced him to confront reality and accept a new order of things in the home. It seems highly unlikely that things will ever return to what they were and that John Morrison will have to reassess where he stands in relation to his wife and perhaps also reassess his role within the family.

(C) JENNY

Although Jenny disappears for much of the play, she plays a crucial role in the plot, especially by providing a resolution to many of its central conflicts and themes. She brings great sorrow to her parents, but in the revised version Stewart highlights Jenny's determined effort to make amends for the suffering she inflicts on them. In her case the perennial conflict between parents and teenagers is given a much more painful, almost tragic aspect by the humiliation she feels over her family's poverty, something she tends to blame her father for. Ironically his attempt to assert his authority over her in Act One only succeeds in hardening her resentment against him, making her defiant and impudent and even more determined to leave home. In this she soon finds a ready ally in the sneering Isa whom she starts to emulate in attitudes and manners, as if temporarily attracted to the defiant female role model she provides.

Her departure in Act Two is an extremely dramatic moment in the play, with a long painful silence after her footsteps fade away, and she thus inflicts even further misery on her mother at the very point where she is already very distressed by the news of Bertie's tuberculosis. Yet in spite of the impact on her parents, Jenny sees leaving home as her only alternative if she is to avoid a similar fate to her mother's. Her desire to seek an independent life as an unmarried woman is therefore a challenge not only to her parents but to the social conventions of the time. In spite of the risks and uncertainties she faces in doing so, Jenny, like her mother, is very determined when she has to be, though at this point she is much more single-minded, and even perhaps very selfish as she rejects her mother's plea to stay, but we can clearly see that she finds it difficult to do so and this tells us that she has not yet become quite as hardened as she pretends.

If her departure is a key moment in the drama, her return home in Act Three is an even more dramatic moment, following on as it does from the very tender scene between Maggie and Lily. It is Christmas Eve and there have been earlier references to the fairy on the Christmas tree. Jenny knocks and enters quietly to be immediately welcomed and forgiven

by Maggie, though she soon faces her Aunt's withering
criticisms. Lily in fact accuses her of playing the good fairy:

> Aye. Dreams. Fair-tales. She went awa an impident wee
> bizzom an she's come back on Christmas eve, kiddin on she's
> a fairy wi a magic wand. (p. 92, SF, p. 70)

Whether we view her return and her generous offer to her
family as convincing, or whether we see it as carrying elements
of the traditional fairy tale ending, there is little about a fairy
tale in what she has had to do to obtain the money she now
has, or in what her mother has to do to ensure it is accepted.
In some ways she is also cast in the role of the returning
prodigal daughter or even the unrepentant Magdalene with
a heart of gold. In the ensuing row we learn that Jenny has
suffered much too, even to the point of considering suicide,
but she is now apparently living happily with someone who
is kind, generous and wealthy.

If she appeared selfish earlier in the play, her generosity
and practicality are now highlighted as it turns out that she
has been saving money to help her family and has taken the
initiative in going to the hospital to find out about Bertie's
condition and also in making the arrangements with a friendly
factor to rent accommodation. In spite of the row with Lily
and her father's unforgiving attitude she once again shows
determination to achieve what she wants, not this time for
herself but for her family as a whole, even if she is offering
something that is regarded as the 'wages o sin' according to
Lily or 'whore's winnins' in her father's eyes.

Whether or not we accept her Aunt Lily's acidic assessment
of her as the Christmas tree fairy 'wi a magic wand', Jenny's
return also has some similarities to the ancient tradition of
the dramatic 'deus ex machina' whose unexpected appearance
at the end provides a kind of solution to their problems
and leads to a resolution of the central conflicts of the play,
especially in offering her mother the chance to finally assert
herself and make a crucial decision that will change their lives
forever. It is also very important to note that once Maggie's
determination has overcome John's resistance, it is Jenny who

takes the initiative in showing her father that she still cares for him by holding one of his hands in both of hers as he sits weeping at the end. Thus in trying to repair the damage she has done to her parents she performs an act of great kindness and love, thereby showing that the human values she learned from them have survived in spite of having to learn the arts of survival in a hard, mean world.

The larger world beyond their tenement may or may not be changing for the better, but their society can be changed and is changing. What both mother and daughter have suffered, and especially what Maggie has to do to force John into accepting Jenny's offer at the end, ensures that things can never return to what they were at the start, as the status quo within the family is simply no longer sustainable. The author is clearly showing that her women have made a few courageous steps in at least trying to change their lives for the better, but in order to do this they have had to start making some important changes in the home and in the family. Ironically however, Jenny's offer of help is only made possible because of Jenny's relationship with a wealthy business man, but it is possibly the only credible way that Jenny could acquire such a large amount of money and it perhaps shows that good can come from an unexpected source and that we should perhaps refrain from being as judgemental as both Lily and John have been.

(D) LILY

At first impression, Maggie's sister Lily also appears rather self-satisfied, self-righteous and judgemental, and she certainly can be at times, but as the play develops we soon see that she is in reality a complex mixture of conflicting attitudes: on the one hand cynical, critical and meddlesome, on the other, kind, caring and constructive. At the start of the play she is harshly critical of the state her sister is in, blaming John for most of it, whereas Maggie feels this is simply part of Lily's warped attitude to men and she is clearly very touchy about any references to her status as a spinster. There are several references to a 'disappointment' in her life (as was common in the years

after the First World War) and how she 'missed the boat' as
regards a man, but, as Mrs Bone cynically comments in Act
Three:

> Considerin the number a boats that sinks, she's as weel
> swimmin alang by hersel. (p. 76, SF, p. 56)

Ironically, although Lily has financial independence and
seems fiercely proud of this, she works in a pub, serving men,
a situation that seems only to intensify her hostility towards
them, as she lumps all men together, dismissing them all as
'dirty brutes' who are really only interested in sex and hence
she blames John Morrison for giving Maggie such a large
family that he cannot provide for. Yet a large part of her
earnings in the pub goes to help her sister and obviously the
Morrisons would struggle without that help. Nevertheless,
we need to remember that she is clearly not very well paid for
her work, as she can only afford a cheap pair of gloves from
Woolworths for Maggie's Christmas present in Act Three.

Unlike Isa, Lily seems quite happy single, does not want a
man in her life and definitely does not wish to end up like her
sister running after a houseful of children. Although most of
her critical comments are made in defence of her sister, her
sharp tongue does stir up quite a few rows that Maggie could
often do without, as she certainly never misses an opportunity
to criticise John who in turn seems to enjoy baiting her,
behaviour that generates a real tension between them. John
regards her as an 'interferin bitch' and warns her near the
end to 'keep oot o' this; it's faimily business,' but her reply,
'Oh I'm no in it; I'm jist an interested spectator' simmers with
sarcastic understatement, as she is certainly far from being
a spectator. Perhaps like many Scots, Lily finds it easier to
criticise or find fault than to show sympathy or affection, but
her caring and constructive side is revealed in the way she
regularly brings food or medicine for the children and in general
supports Maggie materially and emotionally throughout all
her difficulties.

Lily's genuine love for her sister is displayed very clearly
several times in the play, such as where she comforts Maggie

on her return from the hospital in Act Two or in the very moving little scene in the last act where she soothes and caresses Maggie like a child, thus displaying her true feelings towards someone she cares for very deeply. As Maggie confesses to her in this scene, 'whaur wid I be wi'oot ye?' (p. 88, SF, p. 68). In fact the Daily Express's critic, Winifred Bannister, considered the relationship between these two women as 'the best thing in the play'.

'I'm yer sister. Faimly type, me', she tells Maggie (p. 89, SF, p. 68) and this is ironically very true. Notice how when referring to the Christmas decorations she says 'I wish we could have bought a wee tree, though', obviously including herself in the collective 'we' meaning the Morrison family because as she later tells Maggie, she has 'nae weans o ma ain tae keep me aye skint' and Maggie recalls how it was always Lily that did her children's Christmas stockings, almost as if Maggie's children are her substitute children. In spite of all her sharp-tongued comments and criticisms, she embodies close family loyalties and virtues, providing essential help and support when it is most needed.

Although Lily usually prefers to speak her mind regardless of the consequences, she is often perceptive and directly honest. Her warnings about Alex and Isa in Act One turn out to be quite prophetic, while some of her criticisms of John are very much to the point, such as her comments about his reluctance to accompany Maggie to the hospital or his failure to pursue his case for a Council house. When John tells her 'tae keep out o this' in Act Three, her blunt, defiant answer infuriates him:

> Why should I? Maggie's ma sister! An I've had tae fight hauf your battles for ye, John Morrison, or the hale lot o ye would hae been oot in the street mair than once! (p. 94, SF, p. 72)

She is undoubtedly speaking the truth here, though whether she should have said it is another matter. The stage directions tell us that

> *(John cannot answer: his hatred of Lily and her truth turns his mouth to a grim line.)*

Yet at the very end when Maggie regrets saying some of the things she has just said about John, Lily's reply (her last line) sums up much of her character:

Why no? Ye wouldna hae said them if they wisna true.
(p. 96, SF, p. 74)

As well as being irrepressibly outspoken at times, she also possesses a clear-eyed down-to-earth realism and practical common sense, as we see from her comments in Act One like 'it wisnae the bliddy capitalists gie'd you a the weans wis it?' (p. 12) or the reprimand she gives Jenny in Act Three after listening to her talk of suicide or in the way she hurriedly hides the flick-knife in her bag, shortly before this, to prevent Maggie discovering that Alex has probably threatened Isa with it. When John attacks Jenny for having left home and bringing so much suffering to her mother, Lily's reply is scathing:

Well, she's hame noo, an Maggie's happiness wis shinin oot
o her face till you came in wi yer Holy Joe stuff.
(p. 92–93, SF, p. 71)

Ironically Lily has of course just been casting all sorts of aspersions about Jenny's newly acquired wealth, and making sarcastic comments about her 'wee love-nest oot west', but immediately springs to her defence as soon as John starts doing exactly what she herself has been doing, i.e. condemning Jenny, thus repeating what she did with him in Act One after her own criticisms of Maggie. She evidently has a habit of contradicting herself but this also highlights her readiness to defend those she thinks need defending, especially her sister, when she sees them being criticised by those who are too ready to condemn, something she is occasionally prone to do herself.

However, when Maggie finally humiliates John at the end, Lily can scarcely prevent herself from gloating over his defeat, seeing it as a vindication of all the things she has said about him. We are told that Lily stands 'arms a-kimbo, eyes a-gleam' and that she 'laughs coarsely and hugs herself.' In fact at this point she seems to be triumphing much more in John's humiliation rather than in her sister's assertion of her own independence and freedom, thereby revealing her bitterness towards men as almost something ingrained and perhaps rooted in a deep hurt or disappointment in her own past, as hinted at by John. Her behaviour at the end also maybe makes us recall Maggie's criticism of her in Act One:

> Lily, ye're mind's twisted. You cannae see a man as a man.
> (p. 16, SF, p. 8)

Undoubtedly the very dark ending of the original version seemed to vindicate Lily's jaundiced view of men, something that was commented on by several critics and which we have already discussed. By allowing Maggie to overrule her and state her claim to a positive way forward for the whole family, the play's new ending puts quite a different complexion on things indeed, thereby reasserting a more balanced perspective on men and marriage.

Lily is, therefore, a complex, contradictory and very important character who adds a great deal of zest and a few lashings of vinegar to the play. In spite of all her faults, her positive qualities and strength of character are highlighted throughout the play, especially in contrast with the mercenary Isa or the grasping and dishonest Lizzie, Maggie's sister-in-law, as we see how Lily stands up to her poisonous accusations and puts her in her place in Act Two Scene One. There is also no doubt that Lily's voice and her role in the play had its admirers both in 1947 and when it was revived in 1982. The novelist Nancy Brysson Morrison, who was very impressed by the original production, especially appreciated Lily's contribution towards her enjoyment of the play:

> All honour to our namesake (i.e. Maggie Morrison). I personally felt [...] grateful for the antiseptic acidity of Aunt Lily.

Some have seen Lily not only as a highly independent woman, but as almost a caricature of a zealous type of modern feminist who blames men for all the evils of society. She could also be seen as representative of a new kind of female independence that many women gained after more jobs opened up to them during the First World War, though plenty of them already worked long hours in shops or factories or as servants and farm workers for very meagre wages. But Maggie's sister is also representative of a generation of spinsters who lost their young men in the First World War and had little or no choice when it came to men and often had to stay at home to look after other family members, especially elderly parents or grandparents. Those that managed to stand on their own two feet financially by going out to work were sometimes looked on with jealousy by those who did not have that option, while they also undoubtedly posed a threat to some who took a dim view of independent women.

(E) ALEX AND ISA

If John Morrison appears to represent a positive hard-working male identity, his son Alex is presented as the very opposite: weak, indolent, spoiled, sly and dishonest. In contrast to his sister, Alex only uses his family for what he can get out of it, thinks only about himself and readily turns to violence when he cannot obtain what he wants. In fact we are told early in the play that he has a past history of violence, having once attacked Lily with a breadknife and been involved in some other unspecified trouble that had landed him in court (Act One, Scene One, p. 21, SF, p. 12–13).

In the opening scene we also learn from Lily of his gambling successes, though when he has plenty of money, it is all spent on Isa and his family see nothing of him. In contrast to this, when he and Isa are homeless and hard up they move into the Morrisons' house, bringing nothing but trouble. He borrows from his aunt and does not repay her, while he exploits his mother, playing on her sympathy by pretending that he is ill, then pinching pennies from her purse when she is not looking in Act Two Scene Two.

Since taking up with Isa, Alex has graduated from gambling to mugging in an increasingly desperate attempt to stop Isa running off with her new admirer, Peter Robb, who has what she requires, namely plenty of money. Alex is clearly portrayed as a rather pathetic, even despicable figure, reduced, as he frequently is, to a humiliated and grovelling sycophant or enraged to the point of madness where he is prepared to do anything to keep Isa. His Aunt Lily's description of him in Act One Scene One as 'a dirty wee whippet' is also most apt, especially as he has just won money gambling at the dog racing but the metaphor also suggests how thin and sleek or rather 'sleekit' he appears, while also perhaps implying how quick he is at giving creditors, like herself, the slip. He is, therefore, a very difficult character to feel any sympathy for, unless we see him as a poor wee boy lost in a big bad cruel world. Isa pushes him around, calls him a 'rat' and a 'pimple', taunts him for being 'a wee boy running to his mammy' and mocks him for not being able to stand up for himself. Thus we might feel a temporary flicker of sympathy for him because of the way she treats him, although ironically she boasts to Maggie that she has 'improved him'!

When he is finally driven in his desperation to attempt to murder her in Act Three, the play hovers on the verge of tragedy, or rather melodrama, something the original version had no shortage of, and in this version Alex did in fact kill Isa. However in the revised version, the author toned this down considerably as Isa cunningly outwits him and reduces him to 'a sobbing heap.' His final words in the play 'I'll get the baith o them' might threaten violent retribution on Isa and her new paramour, but we very much suspect this is an empty threat which he is totally incapable of carrying out. He is portrayed as neither hardened enough, nor mad enough to kill anyone, at least not yet and that is at least something to his credit, little though it is. We hear no more of him after he runs out to seek revenge and he clearly does not seem to fit into Maggie's plans for a better future.

Yet who is most to blame for the way Alex has turned out? John would appear to be a role model in many ways but he seems to have a poor relationship with a son who accuses his father of always being unfair to him, as if he feels his father has been too strict or critical in the past and never given him the support or encouragement he needs. Whoever is to blame,

and we are unlikely to accept Alex's version of events, there
clearly is not a very positive relationship between father and
son, no doubt accentuated by the generation gap between an
older man used to and proud of working hard and a son who
is used to doing as little as possible and obviously has little
intention of working hard, if he can possibly avoid it. We can
perhaps make some allowance for the fact that he has grown
up in an age of mass unemployment and dire poverty, but
unlike his father, the author does not show him making any
attempt to find real work, though his father does admit that
he has little chance of finding any. Perhaps in some ways they
represent a gulf between an older and newer working-class
or rather non-working-class Scotland.

In contrast to his father, Alex's mother always appears to
have been over indulgent and over-tolerant of his weaknesses
and she finally acknowledges her guilt about this to Lily near
the end of the play. He is Maggie's first child and we see her
over-indulgence of him several times in the play, making excuses
for him in front of the neighbours because he is 'delicate' and
in fact sometimes speaking to him as if he was still a child,
something he invariably uses to his advantage, such as when
he steals from her purse in Act Two Scene Two. Lily tells Maggie
she has 'kept him a wean, tryin tae make up ...' This unfinished
comment suggests perhaps that his mother has tried to shelter
him from a tough world, to make up for the fact that it offers
few prospects and little chance of a decent way of life.

Isa's assessment of him is, of course, much less charitable
but possibly more truthful. She describes him as 'jist a great
big baby' because 'the first yin's aye his mother's big tumphy'
and she thinks that Maggie has never forgiven her for taking
'her wee boy away frae her.' When Maggie accuses Isa, in Act
One Scene Two, of not helping him, her cutting reply is hard
to argue with:

> He wis a rotten tattie lang afore I was daft enough tae get
> landed wi him. (p. 31, SF, p. 20)

When she claims to have 'improved' him, it is unlikely that
she means improvement as a person, but as a streetwise crook

becoming more proficient at earning money the easy way, such as thieving or mugging. He thinks he can find success in the shady world of gambling and bookies but he is not really cunning or deceitful enough to prosper, though he has learned enough of these skills to justify Lily's description of him as a 'rotten wee bastard'. Perhaps the play is suggesting that his rottenness is not so much his mother's fault, as she fears it is, but more the rottenness of a society from which he has learned that animal cunning, dishonesty and violence are the easiest, or only, ways to obtain wealth and 'respect'. Yet even if we accept this viewpoint, the author certainly makes it very difficult for the audience to overlook his faults and failings.

Alex and Isa's relationship is a kind of subplot which shadows the main relationship between John and Maggie, but very much the antithesis of it. In contrast to the Morrisons' traditional marriage, Isa and Alex's relationship could be seen as symptomatic of all that is worst about a fast-changing modern world where relationships do not last and no real commitments or ties are involved. In fact Alex and Isa's relationship is almost entirely mercenary, at least on Isa's part. They return to live with the Morrisons in Act One only out of necessity and they show no appreciation whatsoever that Alex's parents have taken them in when they do not even have a roof over their heads. In spite of this, Isa is far from being respectful towards Maggie and in fact despises the way she slaves for her family. Isa does absolutely nothing to help her, shows no sympathy whatsoever and is also quite unkind to Granny. When Isa makes her first appearance in Act One Scene One, we are told in the stage directions that her eyes 'have a very nasty look' and she really does not change very much, though she is capable of wearing other faces to fool Alex or flatter John.

Like Lily, Isa is fiercely independent, but she is in fact a very different sort of character altogether. Whereas Lily tends to blame men for all the things women have to suffer, Isa is presented as being quite willing to make use of men for her own ends and is clearly in the habit of using her sexuality to obtain what she wants. Very much the 'gallus' tart of the period, Isa displays a tough and ruthless attitude to life in a harsh world that offers her little more than a client does to a prostitute. She wants all the flashy wealth of the popular culture of her time and despises her 'wee nyaff' Alex because he cannot deliver the necessary money to buy the kind of clothes and accessories that sustain her illusions, like fur coats and 'crockydile' shoes. In her tawdry 'film star' clothes she appears to Alex as the sexual ideal of the Hollywood movies in the great era of the 'silver screen'. He feels that as long as he has Isa he still has a chance of being a success and her departure is the final confirmation to him that he is a failure in her eyes. In Act Two Scene One when Alex tries to tell her that he loves her she mocks not only him, but cynically scorns the very idea of believing in love:

Love! Hee-haw! There's nae sich a thing ... No roon aboot here, onyway. Don't kid yersel. (p. 57, SF, p. 41)

In her view, any real human values or emotions are looked on as a sign of weakness and therefore obsolete as they get in the way of the get-rich-quick dreams which seem to offer an escape from the real world of the Depression. Her animal cunning and ruthless self-seeking are the weapons she has developed to fight her way to riches and anything or anybody that stands in the way is dispensable, as Alex ultimately finds to his cost in Act Three. Her outlook on life is simply to look after 'number one', and in this respect she seems very much the product of a rotten society and the glitzy film-star culture of the period which often provided a fantasy escape world from a harsh reality, rather like the celebrity-obsessed media of today.

In contrast to Maggie who has spoiled her son, Isa mocks his dependence on his mother and boasts how, unlike for her,

He'll dae whit I tell him ... I can twist him roon ma little finger. (p. 31, SF, p. 20)

She is very much the dominant partner in the relationship, referring to him as a 'pimple' as if he was her sycophantic servant. Mrs Bone, who is regularly abused by her husband, is hugely impressed by the way Isa bosses Alex about and by the way he fawningly tries to please her and constantly runs after her. Isa seems to have few redeeming features, other than her withering honesty about Alex.

Again we could debate how far we see her toughness as a product of her society or how far she is just presented as hard and predatory by nature, though you might also feel that her character is thus too one-dimensional. Ironically she is a woman who desires a kind of independence from men but who cynically uses her sexuality to obtain what she wants from them. For all that she seems determined not to become trapped in a relationship, she escapes from Alex only to seek another man with more money in his pocket, though, unlike Jenny, we would find it difficult to imagine any appreciation or kindness involved in her new relationship which we can imagine being mercenary and equally temporary. However, unlike Jenny, we could never envisage her using money to help others, while unlike Lily, she would be highly unlikely to seek or wish financial independence through her own honest hard work.

(F) LIZZIE

If Isa's exterior seems as tough as a crocodile skin, Lizzie's is like granite. She is described in the stage directions as a 'hard-faced harridan, about fifty' and even Isa considers her incredibly hard-hearted: 'they dug you oot o a quarry.' (p. 49, SF, p. 35) Whereas we might, at a stretch, be able to view Isa with a sneaking sympathy, perhaps for being landed with Alex, Lizzie is beyond even this. Completely stone-hearted and mercenary, she views her turn to care for Granny as simply an opportunity to make money from her pension, something that Granny complains about early in Act One Scene One, while Mrs Harris vividly describes her notorious meanness in a grotesquely comic image near the end of this scene:

> Yon Lizzie, she'd screw the teeth oot o yer heid if she could get onythin for them in the pawn shop. (p. 26, SF, p. 16)

Indeed Lizzie even emphasises her own hard-nosed business perspective in her own words near the start of Act Two Scene One:

> I'm no takin in naebody tae feed. Folks that canna pay for their meat'll find nae room in ma hoose. (p. 43, SF, p. 30)

She also runs a highly profitable business selling second hand clothes to the poor, lends money to them at exorbitant rates and has also spent time in jail for fraud with a club fund. In many ways she is not unlike some of the bonus bankers and financial swindlers of today who have caused massive unemployment, debt and misery. She embodies all the worst aspects of a raw and ruthless Capitalism driven by a vicious greed which views vulnerable people as ripe for exploitation or disposal when they are no longer productive or too old, like Granny. If her heart is like stone, her tongue is sharp and venomous, something Mrs Bone perceives all too clearly in Act Two Scene One:

> Her tongue's that rotten it'll drap aff yin o these days.
> (p. 46, SF, p. 32)

Lizzie's almost total lack of humanity is neatly summed up in the joke Mrs Bone shares with her friend Mrs Harris earlier in the same scene about her not being surprised by 'anythin human', which clearly implies that Lizzie does not fit into the category of 'human'.

Yet even someone as hard-hearted as her is almost embarrassed by circumstances into displaying a momentary flicker of humanity when Maggie returns from the hospital in Act Two Scene One, distraught with the news of Bertie's tuberculosis. As Lizzie leaves with Granny she says 'sorry about the wean, Maggie,' but the stage directions tell us this is said 'with an effort' as if she is reluctant to say it, or does not know how to, since she normally does not show any sympathy for anyone and, as she hurriedly exits, she reverts to type by blaming Maggie for not taking him to the hospital sooner, as if to imply it is her own fault.

(G) THE OTHER CHILDREN

Whereas the Morrisons' older children play key roles in the drama, their younger children only make brief appearances, as if their occasional presence seems only to demonstrate that the Morrisons have many mouths to feed or to show the effects of poor living conditions on their health. However, there is more to them than this limited though important function. The younger children are not exactly healthy or thriving, but neither are they broken or pathetic, as we often see them squabbling or being chided and even threatened with a skelping. Thus Stewart clearly refuses to sentimentalise the children, as she could so easily have done several times in the play, but instead makes them cheeky, curious, funny, tearful, resilient and gritty children who are very much alive in spite of all their hunger and deprivation, especially Ernest and Edie. In their chirpy back-court speech and in their grubby faces and clothes, the children have the ring of authenticity about them and thereby add a very important element to the drama.

Edie and Ernest are the most prominent or visible of them, but are very much focused on just being children: playing, getting something to eat and grumbling about being washed or having chores to do, always hungry, dirty, the backside hanging out of their 'breeks'. In fact things are so bad in Act One that Edie hasn't even 'got a pair o knickers tae her name'. The youngest children are only conspicuous because of their drying clothing and the noises they make offstage or behind the set-in bed curtain, from where we hear Marina singing or girning at the start of the play. Throughout the play we see the babies' nappies hanging up and also frequently hear them crying, (especially the rickety Christopher) which not only adds to the noise level but also the tension in places, something that formed a key part of the original ending.

Notice too how the children are shown following parental role models. Ernie takes the lead from his father several times in the play, moaning about women and their limitations in failing to understand football or men, and it is highly significant that, when Maggie returns to resume her duties at the end of Act Two, Ernie again copies his father in sitting watching his sister Edie doing her best to help her mother by putting the kettle on and setting the table, while he does nothing. We also see him happy beyond his wildest dreams in the final act: listening to jazz on the new radio, scoring imaginary goals while wearing his long-desired pair of football boots and then bonding with his father as they set off to buy a football for his Christmas. Thus we are shown that gender roles are already well established within the home, even at their young age.

Apart from their older children, the child who causes the Morrisons most concern and has the greatest impact on their lives is young Bertie. We regularly hear his persistent hacking cough in Act One, but he is kept in the hospital from Act Two, Scene One onwards, something that leaves his mother almost inconsolable since tuberculosis was often a death sentence in those days. We never actually see him onstage, only his wee boots which are left lying on the table when Maggie returns from the hospital after he is 'kep in'. In Act Three we learn that he will only have a decent chance of surviving if he has somewhere better to stay, though Maggie has kept the truth about this from John. Thus he is another important motivating factor in Maggie's transformation at the end and it is for him above all else that Maggie forces John into accepting Jenny's offer.

(H) THE NEIGHBOURS

In contrast to other parents in the tenement, the fact that John and Maggie still care about each other implies that they are rather exceptional since there is little evidence of care or affection in their neighbours' marriages, judging by what we hear around them from the garrulous trio of Mrs Harris, Mrs Wilson and Mrs Bone who do not have their own problems or sorrows to seek and whose shouting matches or violent quarrels require fairly regular thuds on the ceiling or floor with a brush.

Thus the neighbours provide a continual series of contrasts and comparisons to the Morrison family, firstly, to reinforce the point that their struggles and family problems are just part of the general pattern of things in this community, but, secondly, to remind us that, no matter how bad things are for the Morrisons, there are others much worse off. We regularly hear or hear about violent bullying or drunken husbands, especially Mrs Bone's, all of which reinforces the point that, in spite of being out of work, the men still exercise male power and control over their wives, perhaps in some cases to compensate for having no control over anything else.

In Act Three when they are all celebrating in Maggie's kitchen, a thud on the floor makes Mrs Bone jump up, 'as if she has been shot', and we soon hear Mr Harris's voice telling his wife 'tae get the Hell oot o it' as he wants some 'atten-shun,' barking this last word almost like a sergeant major. Unlike her friends, Mrs Harris at least puts up some spirited resistance and even defiance, by shouting back up to her husband, 'ask for it politely and ye'll maybe get it!' She may be displaying an element of bravado here, but she also tells her neighbours, 'I'm no needin him ... 'Cept for his wages,' (p. 82, SF, p. 62), a situation that had to be endured by many women, in contrast to Lily's financial independence.

Yet in spite of all their problems, Maggie's neighbours still have enough energy and resilience to enjoy a good gossip and even a laugh about difficulties such as demanding or stupid husbands, matters they can only tell other women about, though somewhat reluctantly or evasively, like the causes of Mrs Bone's regular black eye – due of course to having a bad habit of bumping into things! At times in the play Maggie clearly cannot do without their help, especially to keep an eye on Granny or the children and she has to remain on good terms with them or even bribe them after heated words have been exchanged, as at the end of Act One Scene One.

Certainly the Morrisons' neighbours are very gossipy and inquisitive, but, as Maggie says in Act One Scene Two, 'only rich folks can keep theirselves tae theirselves,' whereas poor folk 'hev tae depend on their neighbours when they're needin help' (p. 33, SF, p. 22) and Maggie definitely cannot do without hers at various times in the play. This kind of supportive network of mutual help and care is traditionally one of the greatest strengths of working-class communities and it is often argued that one of the tragedies of modern society is that more prosperous times have severely eroded such community values and the human qualities that were integral to them (see the discussion of this under **Setting**).

Though sometimes strained, the women's relationships are a vital element in the dynamic of the tenement, reminding us of the importance of a shared female community in their lives. They can be sarcastic, cunning and two-faced, but they also possess, like Maggie and Lily, a down-to-earth realism and common sense as regards some of the important things in life, illustrating another way in which Ena Lamont Stewart reveals her admiration and sympathy for working-class women in general.

'They're no saints, but they are kindly, coarse but kindly', says Maggie in Act Three (a comment that is not very different from how Chris Guthrie sees many of her neighbours in the novel *Sunset Song* by Lewis Grassic Gibbon) but 'as long as you keep on the right side of them,' she hastens to add (p. 82, SF, p. 62). This certainly cannot be said about another female visitor, Maggie's hard-hearted sister-in-law, Lizzie, a skinflint of a relative who grudges taking her turn to look after Granny unless she can make some money from doing so (see section **(F)**, above).

The neighbours also bring an important source of comic relief to the play, such as their breathless description of the collapsed tenement in Act One Scene One, or their discussion of illnesses and men at the start of Act Two, but they are not there only to provide additional amusement. As natural gossips, they are used by Lamont Stewart as commentators on the action to provide information or opinions about the goings on in the building in general and Maggie's house in particular. In this way they act like a Greek chorus at times, but as well as passing judgement on others and often providing moral comment of one kind or another, they are also very much involved in the action, such as looking after Granny and standing up to Lizzie. Also, since they do not always see eye to eye on everything, they provide us with contrasting viewpoints on a variety of topics from domestic issues to the political or more often the politics of the home.

6. MOOD AND TONE

Although *Men Should Weep* is a moving and painful drama about poverty, showing the squalid living conditions of slum dwellers, the tone of the play is far from being monochrome, as the darkness of slum life is lightened by frequent shafts of comedy. Considering the subject matter it may seem rather surprising that there is in fact a great deal of comedy in the play and much of it stems from the women, as if it is a natural part of their defence mechanism. Indeed it is almost as if they just have to laugh at how bad things are in order to keep their sanity, sometimes displaying a kind of black ironic humour and, at other times, a more bitter or stoical variety, both of which testify to the human resilience of ordinary folk coping with the most trying of circumstances.

Their ability to relive and share what is genuinely funny about their own experiences and capture them in memorable expressions or vivid comic images is a kind of art in itself while these moments of shared hilarity also act like a kind of medicine, healing old wounds or making the painful seem less painful. Their love of reductive idioms frequently brings anything pretentious or romantic crashing back down to earth, as where Mrs Wilson says in Act Three, after her La Scala story, that it is nice to look back on 'coortin days' as 'the best' but this is immediately followed by Mrs Bone abruptly bringing them back to the reality of how unromantic their lives actually turned out:

Aye. Guid job we've nae crystal balls, eh? (p. 76, SF, p. 56)

In many ways this ability to laugh at adversity is a very traditional Glaswegian characteristic, embodied above all in the central character Maggie Morrison herself, but also in her neighbours who share a great deal of humour as well as gossip, such as at the start of Act Two and again at the start of Act Three in their banter with Granny or jokes about their husbands or their hilarious account of courting days. When discussing

Maggie's red hat in Act Three, Mrs Harris's comment typifies their vibrant, earthy sense of humour:

> It's tae mind ye o the days when ye first kissed and cuddled doon the dunny. Quite the romantic your John. Mines wouldna hae noticed if I'd met him at Simpson's Corner wi a floral po on ma heid. (p. 75, SF, p. 56)

The neighbours see John's Christmas gift to Maggie of the red hat as a romantic gesture which leads on to Mrs Wilson reminiscing about her own courting days when she was taken to the La Scala cinema:

> I wis that excited didna notice there wis silver paper on ma toffees till I wis hauf-way through the poke! Ma Goad the pain I had in ma stummick! ... Thought I was sent for!
> (p. 76, SF, p. 56).

Lines like the above are almost show-stoppers that would not be out of place in a Glasgow pantomime or music hall comedy, while there are also almost stand-up comic stories or routines like Maggie's mimicry at John's expense in Act One, describing his attempts to cook breakfast or the argument between Maggie and Mrs Harris about whether Mary Harris has 'beasts in her heid'.

Granny is also oddly enough frequently used as a source of humour in a way that is sometimes pitifully comic. Forever lamenting and frequently grumbling, she is a frail, helpless old woman who is totally dependent on her family and it is a moment of real pathos when she is taken away by Lizzie in Act Two. In contrast, Maggie and John habitually make fun of her, but they are never really unkind and she very much prefers to live with them than with the heartless Lizzie.

As a very entertaining comic caricature, her litany of lamentations can be so predictable that the Morrisons just cannot resist some jibes at her expense, such as Maggie's jokes about her being unlikely to be 'drappin deid' or 'ebbin awa' in the opening scene or where John refers to her as 'the aul soor-dook' in Act Three (p. 72, SF, p. 54). In fact at times, they treat her just like another of their children, something that John makes clear in his joke in Act Three about hanging up her stocking for Christmas:

> GRANNY   A stockin? *(She sniggers)* A stockin! Stockins is
>   for weans.
> JOHN   Aye, that's right.
>   (p. 72, SF, p. 54).

Yet although she is physically frail and showing signs of dementia, her tongue is still sharp enough to criticise and complain about the many things she disapproves of, such as the money being spent by the Morrisons on Christmas jollifications, something that makes her sound almost like a comic Granny Scrooge. In effect we very much sense that she actually enjoys being contrary, or thrawn, as if this is just about the only way she has left to express her own individuality, instead of being treated like a difficult or helpless child who is passed on from one family member to another. She is certainly not going to be dancing any 'Heilan Fling' for the neighbours (Act Two Scene One) and she takes great self-righteous satisfaction in voicing her disapproval of Maggie's red hat in Act Three:

> JOHN   We didnae invite your opinion, Granny.
> GRANNY   Weel, I'm giein ye it for naethin. Black wid hae
>   been better ... A red hat! It's no as if she ever
>   sets fit in the kirk door. A croashy bunnet would
>   hae done her as weel.
>   (p. 72, SF, p. 53)

At the same time she does not refrain from saying what she thinks of people who do not meet with her approval, as we see from her comments about Isa at the start of Act Two:

> a tink – Maggie should rin her oot o the hoose.
> (p. 42, SF, p. 29)

She can even be quite perceptive or even cruelly witty, such as in Act Three Scene One where Ernest is asking his father about the ball he promised and she tells John to 'gie him a bat on the ear instead'. Thus, although she may sometimes appear wandered and confused, her mental faculties are far from dormant and she is always suspicious of what people are up to:

there's on-gauns in this hoose (p. 42, SF, p. 29)

Whit are ye up tae, eh? I aye ken when ye caw me Chookie ye're up tae somethin' (p. 83, SF, p. 62)

There are also some very funny exchanges indeed between Granny and the others in Act Three and one of the funniest scenes in the play is where Maggie and Lily have to waken Granny up to put her to bed so that they can 'escape' to the shops for a short while, but as usual she isn't easily cajoled and has to be 'doped' with an aspirin and some vanilla tablet before she is put down for the night, still protesting loudly.

Ultimately her predictable lamentations and warnings almost form a background comical refrain which amounts at times to a parody of a dour, disapproving voice from a grim past, wailing and warning us that we will pay for any pleasures in this life, in contrast to the younger generation who are very much looking for a good time in the here and now. Indeed Granny is almost presented at times, especially in Act Three, as a caricature of a biblical prophet of gloom and doom who forms a counterpoint to the happiness around her and provides a warning that it will not last, though the author is also maybe suggesting that no matter how bad things are at times for everyone, they are never unremittingly bad.

Writing about the importance of humour in Unity Theatre's most successful plays in his introduction to *Scottish People's Theatre*, Randall Stevenson refers to 'a community of language and experience, and a sense of the possibility of laughing off adversity,' which he argued, 'regularly flowed out in this way from stage to audience'. He points out that warmth and humour were often more important than any 'message', political or otherwise and there is no doubt that this certainly holds true for *Men Should Weep*.

Indeed, the *Scotsman*'s critic wrote of the original 1947 production that 'despite the sincerity and bitterness with which the dramatist presents her main argument, sometimes one is moved to think that there is more sugar than pill':

> Here is the Glasgow humour, quick, raw, homely at its best and it is 'put over' with punch and vigour.

Perhaps you might want to consider whether the comedy is at times overdone, by resorting too much to variety theatre quips, cheap laughs or comic caricatures, and whether this is in danger of detracting from the serious message of the play or whether you think that it in fact complements it.

There are also frequent fluctuations of mood throughout the play and comedy is never far from the surface, emerging even at seemingly inappropriate moments, such as Mrs Bone's attempts to cheer Maggie up with her 'they can dae a soarts o things wi lungs' story when Maggie returns from the hospital in Act Two Scene One (p. 51, SF, p. 36), distraught about the news of Bertie's tuberculosis. We even switch from scenes which are painful or violent to moments of great humour and back again, as if tears and laughter, tragedy and comedy are never far away from each other. Even in the moments of hilarity with the neighbours in Act Three, Alex is perched like a restless rooster ready to pounce or take flight at the least little thing – and in fact he attempts to murder Isa in the next scene, while ironically the Salvation Army band is playing 'O come all ye faithful' in the street below! No wonder a *Daily Express* critic referred to 'the see-sawing between comedy and tragedy' of the 1947 version.

The 1947 play certainly contained plenty of both, from the raw comedy mentioned above to the catalogue of disasters at the end which included a murder and the death of the heroine. In contrast the revised version approaches tragedy on several occasions, but draws back from it, just as Jenny draws back from suicide or Alex draws back from killing Isa, but we are still left with no shortage of dark moods, pain and anguish in the drama.

This intermingling of moods is perhaps Ena Lamont Stewart's way of expressing not only a sense of the precarious and unpredictable nature of life under such circumstances but also her admiration for the fortitude and resilience of ordinary Glaswegians battling against the hardships of life in the Great Depression of the 1930s. Ultimately it is a play about survival of the human spirit in adversity and looks forward cautiously, even apprehensively, to the possibility of a better future. Indeed its 'muted optimism' was highlighted by the *Daily Mail* critic Jack Tinkler, who saw it as 'rare in works of such stark social realism.'

His reason for saying this was that 'the bonds of family affection, though never sentimentalised, are nevertheless strong enough to survive most, if not all, the strains put upon them.'

7. STYLE, TECHNIQUE AND STAGING

As well as containing substantial differences in plot, characterisation and tone, another major difference between the 1947 production and the revived 1982 version was in the overall style of performance and the actual staging of the play. In the original version the emphasis was very much on social realism with the actors performing their parts in as naturalistic and authentic manner as possible in order to create 'real life' characters who could almost have walked straight in from the tenements. The production also used a box-set with walls, doors and windows, which was the norm in most productions of the time, and, as you will be able to see from the old photographs of the production, it almost looks like an actual tenement living room / kitchen: poorly furnished and drably decorated, the stage cluttered and space very limited to suggest the cramped and untidy living-space in which people almost fall over each other. All of this certainly created an impression of authenticity of location, atmosphere and mood appropriate to a very realistic play with a grim ending.

However in the 1982 production, the director Giles Havergal, highlighted what he called 'epic stylistic features' of the play which he felt at times required a more non-naturalistic style of acting:

> It seemed to me that the characters were crying to get out of the room and that very often they talked to each other not just in naturalistic dialogue, but they were speaking in a much more epic way.

Though the acting was still rooted in authentic Glasgow voices and mannerisms, the actors were also asked to occasionally modulate the flow of the dialogue, almost as if changing key, and turning aside to address the audience more than other characters, especially during crucial confrontations in the play. For example, during John and Maggie's row at the

end of Act Two, Maggie almost addresses the audience more
than John:

> Aye I've seen yous men lookin for work. Haudin up the street
> corners, ca'in doon the Government ... tellin the world whit
> *you'd* dae if you wis runnin the country
> (p. 61, SF, p. 44)

Or again in her last lines in this act, where her words were
directed straight to the audience:

> I wonder whit kind o a male idiot called indigestion heart-
> burn? Ma Goad – I could tell him whit heartburn is.
> (p. 65, SF, p. 50)

These moments were not sustained long enough to interfere
too much with the natural flow of speech but they often had
the effect of almost stepping aside from the action to comment
on it, in effect the kind of alienation technique associated with
Brechtian theatre, while the neighbours' role as a sort of Greek
chorus, describing and commenting on the action, was also
highlighted much more, again another feature of epic theatre
that helped break the bonds of social realism and naturalistic
acting (See above in Character section).

In addition to this, Havergal also dispensed with the conventional box-set and deployed instead an open, expressionist
style of set, without walls or doors. His set was constructed
around a scaffolding that revealed the other levels in the
building, with other rooms open to view and neighbours
hanging over or out of openings, as if leaning over banisters
or looking out of windows, listening and watching, to suggest
not only an overcrowded cramped tenement as a whole but
also the close interdependence of their lives, plus all their
comings and goings to and from the outside world. As already
discussed, tenement life in those days was very much a world
of open doors (or even open windows) and usually required
the maintenance of good relationships with neighbours from
whom it was difficult to keep any secrets.

Some critics did not like the changes in the revived production to a more non-naturalistic style of acting, especially in Maggie's role, or the use of an expressionist set, but, on the other hand, others, including Michael Billington of the *Guardian*, regarded them as a key aspect that helped transform the play and gave it a larger dimension. It obviously made a lasting impression on him and he summed it up memorably:

> Giles Havergal's production, however, avoids archaeological realism. Geoff Rose's set is a grey pile of dilapidated junk from which the characters emerge like so many ghosts; people watch scenes they are not in; neighbours circle around like swooping birds; make-up is deliberately exaggerated with eyes shadowed by gashes of fatigue; jazz plays off stage. Instead of a period piece we have a brilliant piece of ritualistic theatre that choreographs tenement life without dehumanising it.

Thus by physically opening the set out in this way, the revived version also seemed to open the play up in other ways too, emphasising not only the wider social environment much more, but also the outside world affecting their lives, especially the bigger social, economic and political factors which have a huge impact on their condition. In spite of the focus on the family and the domestic, the outside world is something we are never allowed to forget about because of the frequent references to economic and political issues in the play as well as the popular culture of cinema, radio dance halls and the new jazz craze that has Ernie 'hootin an tootin' at the start of the last act.

Although the play very much suggests that change begins at home and at the individual level, Stewart equally does not allow us to forget that the huge economic and political problems of the 1930s (or today) were not caused by poor people, but they are the ones who suffer most in hard times as they are very much at the mercy of larger forces beyond their control, such as disastrous decisions made by politicians or bankers. As Lily, Jenny and Maggie all demonstrate in various ways, u have to take responsibility for your own life, as far as you can, and cannot just sit around waiting for something to happen. Yet, just as Jenny and Maggie's decisions will bring about change at the individual and family level, perhaps the play also implies that if bad political and economic decisions can cause poverty, likewise different decisions can help to end it. How far do agree with this or do you think this is going too far or reading too much into the play?

8. OVERVIEW OF THEMES

Clearly the main conflicts of the drama centre on the pivotal relationship between Maggie and John and their struggle to cope with all the problems of their family, especially those of their eldest son and daughter, with the climax of each act arising from a bitter family row involving one of these two and one or both of their parents. From these conflicts several sets of contrasting values emerge.

Firstly, what has certainly remained at the core of the play from the original version is the depiction of traditional working-class family and community values of caring and sharing, support and solidarity, represented by Maggie and John's relationship, Lily's relationship with Maggie and also the support of the neighbours. In contrast to this, *Men Should Weep* also depicts the more self-centred values of an amoral kind of individualism engendered by a mercenary society that only values people in material terms, a world where people only look out for themselves and ignore or exploit their fellow human beings. The uncaring, grasping behaviour of characters like Lizzie and Isa seems to be bred by a society that teaches people that in order to 'get on' in a hard world you have to be tough, mean and totally unscrupulous in your attitude to others. It could thus be viewed as a battle between a shared communal set of values and a ruthless type of individualism, symbolised at its worst by Lizzie's exploitation of Granny.

But at the heart of the play we are shown the contrasting values and needs of several generations under the one roof, as the Morrisons attempt to cope with nursing Granny and their younger children, as well as accommodating Alex and Isa. In addition they are struggling to come to terms with the growing gulf between their more traditional values and that of the eldest, Jenny, who is increasingly ashamed of her background and determined to escape from the squalor of an overcrowded home and a dead-end job. In some respects Jenny represents the desire of a younger generation to break away from the constricting hold of the family and its values, in order to seek their own way in life and to find something better in the world than what their family or community has to offer.

In addition the play reveals conflicting attitudes to marriage, motherhood and above all the gender roles and norms within the family and in society as a whole. Maggie and Lily have diametrically opposed views on men and marriage, the former believing in the traditional view that marriage is a life-long commitment for better or worse and that her large family is a price well worth paying for the love she and John still share. In contrast, Lily is very cynical about marriage and all that it involves for women and she scoffs at Maggie's claim she is paid with love. Lily is proud of being an independent woman, though ironically she works in a pub serving men and views all men as 'dirty beasts', claiming she would never put up with slaving to such a brute and his brood of children.

Both Lily and Isa make scathing criticisms of the Morrisons' married life, the former blaming John for reducing Maggie to 'living in a slum an slavin efter a useless man an his greetin weans', while Isa teases John with suggestions about all the things he could do if he was not 'pinned down' by a wife and family. Clearly these issues were there from the start, but there is no doubt that the issues of gender roles and expectations within the traditional marriage were brought into much sharper focus by the revised version of the play, something that profoundly affects the overall balance in terms of theme and tone.

Closely related to this conflict, the play also highlights the contrast between a kind of superficial 'respectability' based on conventional moral attitudes regarding sex and marriage and a more honest, and arguably more genuine, kind of morality. For example, it was not then the norm for a young woman to leave home before she was married and co-habitation outside marriage would definitely have been regarded by most as 'immoral.' Thus John is very worried about what the neighbours will think of Jenny's behaviour and, for all her cynicism about marriage, Lily is still, initially at least, very judgemental and disapproving of Jenny's behaviour.

Maggie and John do not attend church but their moral values, and even Lily's, are still essentially based on a mixture of traditional religious values and the values or norms of 'respectable' society of that time. Yet it is not only the younger generation, like Jenny or Isa, who challenge conventional morality. Maggie herself is finally driven to challenge the hypocrisy underlying a kind of 'respectability' based on a moral code that was still essentially Victorian and male-dominated.

If the original production was perhaps centred more on the social and political issues of inequality and poverty, the revived version, while still concerned with these issues, undoubtedly focused more sharply on issues of gender and morality at the heart of the play, forcing us to consider not only the evils of poverty but also the harm caused by male chauvinism and abuse, as well as the detrimental effects of rigid social conventions, gender roles and expectations.

Arguably Stewart's revised version adopts a much more balanced, un-dogmatic perspective on these issues as the play does show that some of the problems faced by her characters are not simply caused by their social and economic conditions but by themselves and likewise it does not suggest that all of the women's problems can be blamed on men as some of the nastiest characters in the play are in fact women. In other words it does not just offer simple causes or solutions like some of Unity's pre-war dramas.

Therefore, while the play reveals the human cost of a very unjust society which allows the poorest to suffer most from the failures of the system, it also probes the human strengths and weaknesses at the heart of the struggle for survival by focusing not only on the problems faced by the family as a whole but the tensions and conflicts generated within the family itself, especially the demands placed on the mother of the family, Maggie Morrison, a resilient and courageous matriarch, a sort of Mother Courage of the Gallowgate (a district in the East End of Glasgow). *Men Should Weep* still has much to say about the human cost of poverty in any place at any time, but it is also a powerful and very relevant drama about family, community, love, kindness, charity and cruelty, desperation and dignity, grace and greed, hope and humiliation, lies and truth and many other things beside, but above all it is theatrical testament to the human spirit triumphing over adversity and despair in a very precarious world.

9. CONCLUSION

Men Should Weep is undoubtedly a powerful and moving drama, or even a tragi-comedy about a time of great injustice and suffering as experienced by people in one very particular time and place: Glasgow's slum dwellers of the pre-war period. However, some have seen it as only an interesting and entertaining period piece about poverty in 1930s with little or no relevance to life today. How far do you accept this critical view or do you agree with a more generous assessment that Ena Lamont Stewart succeeds in transcending the original time and place of her work to produce a memorable dramatic statement about families in poor societies the world over and about the role of women in any society and thus her play acquires a genuine universal and timeless appeal?

10. RECENT REVIEWS

Reviews of both the 1947 and 1982 revival have occasionally been referred to throughout but the play continues to be performed, and it is worthwhile searching online to read how the play has been received more recently. The 2010 reviews by **Paul Mason** (BBC *Newsnight* archive) and **Philip Fisher** (British Theatre Guide) are recommended, as is the 2001 review by **Irene Brown** (Edinburgh Guide).

Try to see a performance if you get the chance, as any play only really comes alive in front of a live audience. If you do, try writing your own review, but remember that theatre is a live art and that even the best productions have good and bad nights – as do reviewers, no doubt for other reasons!

Lightning Source UK Ltd.
Milton Keynes UK
UKOW06f1441260915

259313UK00001B/15/P

9 781906 841256